LOVES, DELIGHTS, & ORGANS

Alphonse Allais
Translated from the French by Doug Skinner
164 pp., trade paperback; $14.95
Black Scat Books
ISBN 978-1-7379430-9-9

The master absurdist is back in this madcap collection of stories, fables, hoaxes & jokes — pataphysical fun for the literate layabout. This first English translation features 47 sublime textual specimens — PLUS six additional stories, a rousing introduction, and enlightening notes on the translation by Allaisian scholar Doug Skinner. If you've yet to discover the bizarre world of Alphonse Allais, you're in for a treat.

"Allais comes across as a very modern writer, and his work as an experimental enterprise which is exemplary in many ways... it is also quite possible to invoke such writers as Raymond Queneau, Italo Calvino, and Jorge Luis Borges."
—Jean-Marie Defrays

STRANGE FRUIT
& other plays
Harold Jaffe
A Black Scat Paperback Original
144 pp., $14.95
ISBN: 978-1737371151

This collection of Harold Jaffe's short, one-act plays is exceptionally diverse. The nine innovative dramas feature Billie Holiday & Lester Young; Antonin Artaud & Georges Bataille; Marilyn Monroe & Marlon Brando; Samuel Beckett; condemned prisoners in Texas making their final statement before execution; Israelis & Palestinians in life-or-death dialogue; Charles Manson unleashed; Jimi Hendrix, Janis Joplin & Jim Morrison burning it at both ends; & the potently satirical "Splish Splash," exploring gender discord.

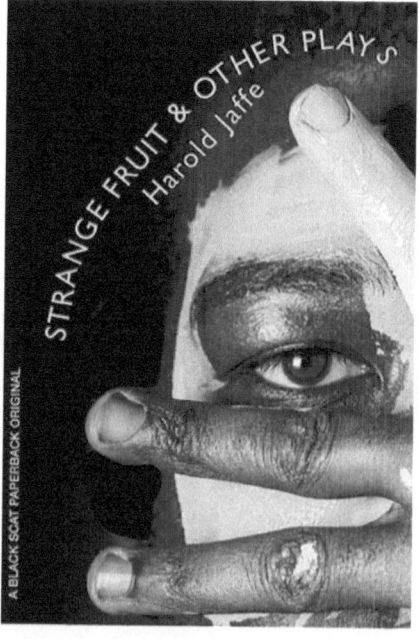

BLACK SCAT
review

NUMBER 24

BLACK SCAT REVIEW is an international journal of the arts, published irregularly in Northern California.

Editor:
Norman Conquest
Contributing Editors:
Derek Pell; **Nile Southern**;
Farewell Debut

–Second Printing–

F + U ÷ N – H + O – U ÷ S + E

BACK ISSUES
The following issues of BSR are available:

Black Scat Review #1 (reprint edition)
Black Scat Review #11
Black Scat Review #18
Black Scat Review #19: The Ecstasy Issue
Black Scat Review #20: Black Humor
Black Scat Review #21: Travel
Black Scat Review #22: Errata
Black Scat Review #23: Wordplay

[ANTI-CONTENTS

UNDER THE BIG TENT:

Mark Axelrod; Tom Barrett; David Berger; Norman Conquest; R J Dent; Muriel Falak; Eckhard Gerdes; Richard Gessner; Alfred Jarry; Richard Kostelanetz; Amy Kurman; Mantis; Kate Meyer-Currey; Bob McNeil; Lillianne Milgrom; Lance Olsen; Paul Rosheim; Doug Skinner; Nile Southern; Jim Yoakum.

CHEM TRAILS
Mantis

"IT'S ALL ON THE *INSIDE*..." the Barker cooed as the mall audience pushed towards his booming voice. Biff Barker was the last in a long line of chem-trail Barkers—these 'doomsday tickers' who could narrate through your damaged DNA strands like it was *Moby Dick*. The twinkling window displays illuminated Biff's sweaty face in day-glo hues making him like talking playdough.

"See *here*," he said, pointing down towards the hunched specimen, "a man consumed by his own depravities—his bag of skin holds a steaming potpourri of ebbing, flowing, inventory: tell-tale traces of the *worst* America has to offer!"

Women with strollers and those expecting ebbed forward with determination—a Chem Trail exhibition was always sobering—especially for those of child-bearing age.

"See HERE!" the Barker practically screamed now, coaxing the twisted man to mount the stage, "a human body so *overwhelmed* by modern times, that his every exhalation is imbued with the sickly data foretelling his own demise. Come up here, my boy—don't be shy. Lay your breath upon my chem-trail *mirror*."

As the crooked man hopped up the steps, the crowd lurched forward—keen to bear witness to any strange new talisman. As if by magic, the Barker revealed a simple hand-mirror, holding it up to the man's face. Upon two breaths, the collection of screens upon the stage lit up, indicating all manner of shifting weirdness and angry calculations.

Trace elements of the 'Big Ten' began pinging wildly, the sounds of toxic alarm attracting the kids in the crowd to move closer. With benzene on high, red-flashing klaxons announced more trouble in situ: CADMIUM, LEAD, ARSENIC, MERCURY, DIOXINS... and some new-fangled, free-floating culprits: PHTHALATES, CHLORINATED MICRO-PLASTICS, PFAS, BISPHENOLS, of known and as yet unclassified natures.

"SEE HERE the hidden ravages of Man: a whopping 20 grams of microscopic tire chafe!? Tell me, lad, tell me," the Barker stooped, shouting into the man's face, "how on *earth* did you come across it in these numbers—or, rather, how did *they* come across *you?!?*"

Taking the Barker's mic, the man spoke oddly, like a doll whose voicebox had blown—the pull-cord cracked and jumping, "Just *walking* the streets of this cursed city," he said, "day in, day out... The *chafe* lives within me!" and just then, a crazy smile seemed to hold forever on both men's faces. This shoeless, apparently homeless man, wearing white lab coat, hipster beany and clearly nothing else, suddenly sprang into action, expertly switching the computerized instruments and screens upon the stage—a world he clearly knew intimately. The magnified images of cellular activity hypnotized all who watched, as mitochondria did tarantellas, live cloud-chamber photography revealed slow motion vapor spores exploding in sienna, and gangs of spikey nebulae clearly itching for a fight fueled this party of insurrection that floated willy-nilly through the churning heat of his blood.

"What we have here," the Barker concluded, "is a *living record* of every brain-barrier transgression violently wrought upon this *North American* man. Tritium in the water—that's right, folks: RADIO-NUCLEIDS! And a healthy dose of good old-fashioned lead! Advertisements for himself? Or for the corporations that relentlessly spurted into him? The utter polluting of his mind and spirit—indeed the soul of this nation... This man has suffered, and *documented* his condition well for years! See here... THE DOCUMENTED MAN!"

At that, the DM stood in a small spotlight the Barker switched on, and took a bow. A sudden release of excrement from his backside was caught by a previously unseen child—perhaps his very own, who held the big zip-lock with a long pool-cleaning pole—catching it like a slab of old rotten butterflies, slipping into the sad net.

A reporter from *Cancer Alley Gazette* rushed forward, making eye-contact with the Barker and whispered, "how much... for an *exclusive?*" The Documented Man was a whirlwind of activity now, moving from station to station: drawing blood, cutting hair follicles into petri dishes, scraping his fingernails with a razor, tossing the steaming hot excrement bag into a slow-bake analysis chamber.

The Barker ignored the reporter, as they were live-streaming now, and began his big finish—passing around an old-style top hat for tips, legal fees, medical expenses, funeral costs and the like.

"It's all on the INSIDE... of *him!*" The Barker ejaculated, "SEE the crazed cellular activity inside the most litigious man in history—a man wronged every moment of every day of his God-forsaken life! Perhaps even *you* afforded him some tresspass—when you carelessly allowed those three tablespoons of *gasoline* to hit the median of that pumping station isle on your way here—the winds just so, *forcing* him to catch a cancer-causing whiff of the juices of our climate's ruin... Did he get your plate number? Stingray your iPhone's GPS? *You bet!* It's certainly *possible...* This could be the day you find out, whether you'll be in *court* with the Documented Man... Look here!" A screen lit up with thousands of names and so-called infractions, scrolling at random, incessantly:

1.25.35; Mark Parker, Brooklyn; exhaled cigarette smoke my way—asshole!

2.22.28; Emily Wishbone, Manhattan; perfume cloud—fucked me up good!

7.28.31; Zac Zajak, Colorado Springs; left car idling for 30 mins—WTF!

And on, and on…

Illuminated by lights and screens abuzz, the DM fidgeted with his infernal machines: tiny modems, air-sensors, noise detectors, micro-gram scales, caustic powders, testing pods—as if he were a turntablist in mid-concert.

"He checks his vitals every 10 minutes. You're in luck to bear witness to this steadfast ritual of the Documented Man. He's been taking such samples every day of his life since… since… the *Accident*… exposing him to 10,000 picocuries of radiation at the tender age of 12."

An EZ-bake style oven opened up with a ping, and the DM studied his toasted shit sample as if reading the future from an up-ended Greek coffee cup. The audience scanned his face, looking for some kind of recognition… Good? Bad? *What?* And as the results began scoring heavily, the DM cracked his crooked smile, and, twisting his head around oddly, suddenly revealed his creeping paralysis, and the extreme difficulty he had withdrawing from his pocket the small notebook on which he made an urgent series of scratch marks.

"He's *onto* something now," the Barker said excitedly, "more… *Documentation!*" As the tiny pen-camera switched on its feed, the DM's scrawl identified someone in the crowd:

EXPOSURE ALERT: 12:42PM, April 12, 2034: 160ppm carbon monoxide from diesel, parked SUV, origin: Commerce City, Colorado, concentrations Mutagenic gases and particulates: benzene, formaldehyde, sulphur, approx. 10,000 polycyclic aromatic hydrocarbons. Airborne mercury, lead, arsenic. Duration: 103 seconds.

"Good lord!" blurted Barker Biff, "whoever left your motor running, *you-are-fucked!*"

Panic spread across the mall, infecting stores in all directions, as the Documented Man looked up to the crowd with a hurt weasel kind of face—a face that said: 'you injured me—and I will *get* you one day!' It was toxic telepathy, and many mentally ran through all the noxious messes they'd casually created that might have affected DM, and might be plaguing his mind now or appear in his little book, or his web tabulation of 'forever chemical' exposures. Phosphates, perfumes and Blue Lake #5 from the laundry from yesterday (had they made sure to use the non-scented?), the wastewater treatment plant's hiccup…County-wide exposures—always the costliest… Or was it those extended farts of pure, meat-laced methane a masked woman in the audience had demurely expunged just moments earlier—might the DM have added her offending odors to the catalog of climate catastrophe he was famous for compiling? raising the temps, and presumably shortening the stretch of his documented life?

"You, madame," the Barker accused, "is that coat *synthetic?*"

DM and Barker looked crazily at her now, their eyes screwing into her jacket…

"If so, you *may* want to leave this room now, or be held to account by the Documented Man for the 'FOR-EVE-R' CHEMS now leaching into *his* bloodstream–the wafts are live-streaming today, registering with every court in the land the world over."

"Good Lord," the woman said, throwing a ten-dollar bill towards the upended hat as she scurried away.

"What's the estimated dollar amount of the DM's lawsuits pending worldwide?" the Reporter asked—backing away, worried his own puffy jacket might be reeking of chemical content or slave labor.

"Well, let's see… Documented Man… what's the *damage?!?*"

With a flourish, the DM revealed a small TV, framed in red velvet curtains as a ticker-tape parade of exposures fell *Matrix*-like down the screen:

DOCUMENTED MAN'S TOXIC EXPOSURES
SUITS PENDING (WORLDWIDE)

Hundreds of thousands of recorded infractions and myriads of measured toxicity tabulated the effects in parts-per-million in a variety of cryptic contexts: CHEMICAL, PHYSICAL, MENTAL, SPIRITUAL, and SOUL-SUCKING—the tables danced upon the screen as the Reporter's pen whirled furiously, trying to hopelessly capture some of it:

BOGATA: 5.23.1996	OIL SPILL FUMES	CHEVRON	.0027	NOXIOUS BREW	PHYS
NIGERIA: 6.12.2033	OIL SPILL	CHEVRON	1.006	TOXIC STEW	CHEM
NYC: 12.22.2021	IDLING TRUCK	RYDER	22MINS	CLOUD	SOUL
LOS ANGELES: 11.27.00	NEIGHBOR	MONSANTO	INHALATION	PFAS	CMPS,SS–BINGO!

"Some say he goes *looking* for trouble," the Barker pitched, "others say he has a knack for *attracting* it... In any event, see here, the most horribly-wronged, well-documented man in history! As Ralph Nader himself recently observed, the DM has single-handedly *inverted* the age-old adage: *privatize the wealth, and socialize the risk!*"

For his closer, the Documented Man always asked the same thing. With belabored breaths, and his sickly, wheezy-voice, he croaked: "Will someone please bring me... *a glass of water?!?*"

The Barker looked around, pleased that a child of no more than eight was already making her way forward with just such a glass, handing it to the DM with tremulous hands. The Doc'd Man smiled his otherworldly smile at her, took one drink, and half-closed his eyes as the machines and his mind began to whirr.

"See now, how the Documented Man, and all his carefully calibrated computer-aided machinery *deconstructs* in real time the liquid litany of litigational ligatures his own tortured soul has accepted from this lovely child. A GLASS OF WATER has been proffered, and the potential adverse health-effects on his person are now... *in effect*. Let the Municipality stand... *on notice!*"

As the DM submerged his homemade prod into the glass, the wires connected to his computer array began to vibrate and constrict—as if protesting the contents coursing through their capillaries.

With a furrowed brow displaying utmost seriousness and consternation, the Barker wound-up for the final blow: "Ladies and gentlemen, the Documented Man has taken a sip of *water*, brought by this cherubic, virginal child. *Water from our community*... water, I say, that undoubtedly will have traces of *who-knows-what* that will be of an adverse nature to the DM's well-established sensitive disposition... Some polyfluoroalkyl 'forever' substances... Hello? Who is responsible? Only the Documented Man will find out—and tell us he will... As he writes now, the time, place and moment, and, uh... what's your name girl?—"

"Sally Lambkins," the girl intoned solemnly—her mother quickly smothering her mouth closed—too late.

"Yes, the time, place, moment and *manner* of the exposure... it's all in his *little book*, you see... and we'll probably all be paying the piper 'ere long—as DM makes his rounds..."

"It's not our fault!" someone screamed from the back. "He's a hypochondriactic psychopath!"

"Yeah, I'm sick, too! Chlorination sucks! What the fuck!"

"It's the water company! The wastewater treatment plant! Write *them* down!"

"Not our fault!! Not our fault! NOT OUR FAULT!"

As the crowd seemed on the verge of storming the stage and pummeling DM—he calmed the scene with a crooky-voiced promise: "Those responsible shall be *revealed*...and *held to account!*"

And with that, the curtain closed, and Biff Barker quietly shooed the addled folks out of there, keen to make ready for the new crowd.

"Come back next week," he cajoled, "to see what happens when our Documented Man meets... The *Undocumented* Woman!"

THE CRUCIFIXION CONSIDERED AS AN UPHILL BICYCLE RACE

Alfred Jarry

Translated from the French by R J Dent

P ilate, the starter, pulled out his clepsydra or water clock, a move which made his hands wet, unless he had surreptitiously spat on them. He gave the start signal.

Jesus got off to a good start.

In those days, it was customary, as reported by the renowned sports commentator, Saint Matthew, to whip the racers at the start, in the same way a coachmen whips his horses. The whip both stimulates and provides a hygienic massage.

Jesus, at the peak of fitness, raced ahead, but he immediately got a flat tyre. A circle of thorns punctured the entire circumference of his front tyre.

Nowadays, in the shop windows of bicycle dealers, we often see a reproduction of this veritable circle of thorns being used as an advert for puncture-proof tyres. Unfortunately, Jesus's was an ordinary track single-tube.

The two thieves, who were obviously working together, took the lead.

It is not true that there were nails. The three shown in the pictures are parts of the so-called 'rapid-change' tire iron.

Although it is advisable that we begin by recounting the accidents, before we do that, we will briefly describe the machine.

The bicycle frame in use today is a relatively recent invention. We saw the first frame bicycles in 1890. Previously, the body of the machine consisted of two crossed tubes joined together. This was what we called the right-angle or cross frame bicycle.

So Jesus, after the puncture, continued up the hill, carrying on his shoulder his bicycle frame, or if you will, his cross.

We have several photographs of the contemporary engravings that depict this scene. But it seems that the sport of cycling – following the well-known accident which so grievously ended the Passion race and which was made topical again, almost on its anniversary, by the similar accident of Count Zborowski on the La Turbie course – was banned for a while by state decree.

This explains why some illustrated magazines, reproducing the famous scene, featured rather fanciful bicycles. They confused the machine's cross frame with that other cross with the straight handlebars. They represented Jesus with two hands spread apart on his handlebars. Let us note in connection with this that Jesus cycled lying flat, a position often used by cyclists to reduce air resistance.

Note also that the frame or the cross of the machine, like some current wheel rims, was made of wood.

Some people have insinuated, erroneously, that Jesus' machine was a draisienne, but that is a very unlikely machine for an uphill race.

According to the old cyclophile hagiographers, Saint Brigitte, Gregory de Tours and Irenaeus, the cross was fitted with a device which they call 'suppedaneum'. It is not necessary to be a great scholar to translate this as 'pedals'.

Lipsius, Justinian, Bosius and Erycius Puteanus describe another accessory, one which was first reported by Cornelius Curtius in 1634 and is still in use on Japanese crosses: a projection of wood or leather on the cross frame, on which the cyclist sits, as though on horseback: obviously a seat or saddle.

These general descriptions, moreover, correspond to the current

Chinese definition of the bicycle: 'A small mule which is led by the ears and moved forward with kicks.'

We will shorten the story of the race itself, for it has been described in numerous works and depicted in sculpture and painting, and in 'ad hoc' monuments.

There are fourteen bends in the rather difficult uphill Golgotha course. It was on the third bend that Jesus came off. His mother, who was in the stands, stood up in alarm.

Simon of Cyrene was an excellent trainer. His function would have been, if not for the thorn incident, to have ridden in front of Jesus to act as a sort of windbreak. Instead, he offered to carry the machine.

Jesus, although wearing nothing, was perspiring heavily. No one is really sure if a spectator wiped his face, but it has been verified as gospel that the reporter Véronique took a snapshot with her Polaroid.

The second fall took place at the seventh turn, on a slippery paving stone. Jesus skidded for the third time, as he bumped over a rail on the eleventh bend.

The Israel demi-mondaine contingent waved their handkerchiefs as the racers passed them at the eighth.

The deplorable incident that we know so well took place at the twelfth bend. Jesus was by this time neck and neck with the two thieves. We also know that he continued the race airborne… but that's another story.

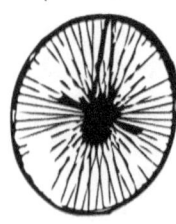

FUNHOUSE

Paul Rosheim

to V. Kamensky

rejoICE

stinkards Emerge from caves

knowing Da *universe* slleMS

D ℼ A ℼ B

fUNhouse mirrors ina would

face **2**
face

COLONOSCOPY

w v y i E §

a e l n s

eXtraTerrestristal hotDOG

sculpted lewd HERon flieR

knot *eclip*Sing

con | cave | **merge**
vex

talking derrière window

———shIFting fur louverS

back pORch *romance*———

no longer afraid to die

EGYPTIAN
Paul Rosheim

COMPULSIPERVERSITY

NOwhere through — avardoCARAVAN

RONDE — campFIRE fights like

CATSEYES — days & nights hypnoTIZED

lovesong **V** nevereND

travelerS   CENTurine

Face pAINTed dandies midelBOWties

DANCE like hell mouth TOURney

₪ SaNTaTaNGO with COWS ₪

INHABIT THIS — sPace for eTERNity

CONNYsewers suitEd for wOK

ReCycLE — CORK

kiss

BLUE —THUNDER BENDER

Hydroglyphs up wombatwalls

AEROplane cLIMBs — snowflight

Oeuvre EARTHquAKES — in vALES

FLY INTO ABSOLUT BEING

FUNHOUSE MIRROR
Norman Conquest

Marcel meets Gertrude

THE POTATO FARM
Doug Skinner

August entered the Camisole Tavern and approached Bud and Paulette, who were sipping porter at the bar.

"I'm starting a new business," he announced, his face flushed with excitement.

"You could say hello first," remarked Paulette.

"Hello," said August.

"And what is it?" Bud asked.

"It'll make me as rich as a king," said August. "I'll have vast wealth at my disposal, and won't have to borrow small sums from my friends."

"And what is it?" Bud asked again.

"A potato farm," August said.

"What a dumb idea," Paulette replied.

"Far from it," said August. "Just tell me, what's in that bowl?"

"Potato chips," said Bud.

"Which," said August, "are not made from carrots, or buckwheat, or some other agricultural product, but from potatoes. Potatoes can be boiled, baked, fried, and mashed, even by an inexperienced cook. They sell like hotcakes. In fact, you can make hotcakes from them too."

"We know all that," said Paulette.

"You don't even need yeast," added August.

"True enough," said Paulette, "but you know nothing about farming.".

The bartender, a gaunt and wizened man named Collier, glared at August. "Buying a drink, or just disturbing the peace?" he asked.

"I'll have a small vodka," replied August with a smile. "That's made from potatoes too!"

"Yes, we know," said Paulette.

Collier set a glass before August, and retreated to his paper at the end of the bar.

"Here's to my new career," crowed August, brandishing his drink.

"You know nothing about farming," Paulette repeated.

"I can learn," August said. "How much are potato trees, anyway? Do they sell them by the dozen, or is it all metric now?"

"Potatoes don't grow on trees," said Paulette.

"They grow underground," added Bud.

"In the dirt?" asked August.

"Of course," said Bud.

"You mean you have to dig them up and wash them off?" asked August..

"Of course," said Paulette.

"And you have to water the part above ground, and keep all the bugs off," said Bud.

"That I don't mind," said August. "But I draw the line at rooting in the dirt like a pig, or washing things off like a raccoon."

Collier looked up from his paper with a scowl. "What's wrong with pigs?" he snapped.

"Nothing," said August, "but I was hoping to stroll around the orchard with a basket, and pick them from the branches."

"That's not how it works," said Bud.

"But if they grow underground," said August, "how do you know when they're ripe?"

"They don't get ripe," said Paulette, "just bigger."

"But you can't tell how big they are when they're buried," August objected.

"No," said Bud.

"Why not plant them upside down?" asked August. "Then you could see them."

"They'd die," explained Bud.

"Why not plant them in a glass box, then?" asked August.

"The dirt would still hide them," explained Paulette.

"What about hydroponics?" asked August.

"You could grow a few that way, but it's not commercially viable," said Bud.

August sat silent for a moment, sipping his vodka.

"You've given me a lot to think about," he remarked quietly. He paid Collier for his drink, and left the bar.

"Everyone jeers at pigs," muttered Collier.

A year later, Bud and Paulette were again sitting in the Camisole Tavern, sipping porter. A new bartender now read his paper behind the bar, but otherwise little had changed.

It was a very different August, however, who strode into the darkened bar. He was leaner, tanner, and his eyes shone with a new sense of purpose.

"Hello," he said to Bud and Paulette.

"Why, it's August!" exclaimed Paulette.

"Hello, August," said Bud. "What's new?"

"I don't know if you remember," said August, "but last year I told you I was starting a potato farm."

"I don't remember," said Bud.

"Me neither," added Paulette.

"Well, that farm is now a reality," said August.

"Congratulations," said Paulette.

"And I'd like to show it to you," August added. "Will you do me the honor?"

Bud and Paulette exchanged a glance, and Paulette shrugged

her shoulders.

"Sure, why not?" she replied. "It's a nice morning for it."

She and Bud paid their tab, and followed August out the door and down the street.

"How big is your farm?" asked Bud.

"Pretty small," answered August.

"Is it profitable?" asked Paulette.

"Not yet," August answered.

They came to a bungalow, where August unlatched the gate. "It's in the backyard," he said.

Behind the house, he showed them a small plot with a dozen wilted plants.

"This is the first dozen," he announced.

"This is more like a garden than a farm," said Paulette.

"Rome wasn't built in a day," said August.

An elderly man came out the back door, a flyswatter in his hand.

"Why, it's Collier!" Bud exclaimed.

"Hi, Collier!" said Paulette.

Collier looked at them blankly.

"We were regulars at the Camisole," said Bud. "Don't you remember us?"

"Nope," said Collier.

"I don't like to get my hands dirty," explained August, "so Collier does the digging."

"I like it," said Collier. "It brings back memories of the years I spent wallowing in the mud."

"Huh," remarked Paulette.

"He digs up the potatoes every day, to see how they're doing," said August. "They don't get ripe, you know, just bigger, but you have to check to see if they've grown enough to be commercially viable."

"That can't be good for the plants," said Bud.

"That's what I tell him," said Collier, "but he won't listen."

"It's the only way to see them, since they grow underground," explained August. "You can't plant them upside down, or use hydroponics."

"Have you read any books about potatoes?" asked Paulette.

"No," said August.

"Any pamphlets from the Department of Agriculture?" asked Bud.

"That would be plagiarism," August replied.

"No it wouldn't," said Paulette.

"Those things are published to teach people," sad Bud.

"It might not be technically illegal," August replied, "but I'd like to avoid even the appearance of impropriety."

Collier swatted a mosquito on a dead plant.

"You have to keep the bugs off," August explained..

"Well, it was nice seeing both of you," said Paulette.

"Good luck with the potatoes," said Bud.

"Thanks for the visit," said August.

"Goodbye," said Paulette.

"Keep in touch," said Bud.

They left the yard and returned to the bar.

A year later, they were again sitting in the Camisole Tavern, again sipping porter. It was even the same brand, since they knew what they liked. Yet another bartender now read his paper where Collier and his successors had once sat, but otherwise little had changed.

Collier entered, and walked up to the bar.

"Are you Bud and Paulette?" he asked.

"Why, it's Collier!" exclaimed Bud.

"We were regulars when you worked here, and we saw you last year with August," said Paulette. "Don't you remember?"

"Nope," replied Collier, "but August described you."

"How is he?" asked Paulette.

"Is he still growing potatoes?" asked Bud.

"The business is booming," said Collier, "ever since I took over as manager. August is a good man, but he has no head for business."

"So you're doing well?" asked Bud.

"We bought a plot of land upstate, and I convinced him not to dig up the plants all the time," said Collier. "We now market a line called Pot o' Gold. Every bag's got potatoes in all the colors of the rainbow: red, yellow, and blue, with yams for the orange, and purple ones for the indigo and violet. Nobody can tell the difference between indigo and violet. For the green ones, we just leave yellow ones out in the sun until they're bitter and toxic. I brought a bag for you." He pulled a mesh bag from his duffle bag.

"Thank you," said Bud.

"August said to give you this," Collier added.

"Why, that's him on the label," said Bud.

"Yup, that's him," said Collier. "He wears that costume for personal appearances."

"Well, best of luck," said Bud.

"Give our best to August," said Paulette.

"Bye," grunted Collier as he left.

A year later, Bud and Paulette were once again sitting in the Camisole Tavern, once again sipping their favorite brand of porter. Yet another bartender now read his paper behind the bar, but otherwise little had changed.

August walked into the bar, and right up to Bud and Paulette.

"Hello," he said.

They stared blankly at him for a moment, then Paulette said, "Why, it's August!"

"I didn't recognize you in that costume," said Bud.

"Collier and I designed it for the potato bag," explained August. "To go with the Pot o' Gold and Rainbow idea."

"Now I remember," said Bud.

"I guess that helps establish the brand," said Paulette.

"Do you two still have that farm?" asked Bud.

"No," said August. "Collier's a good man, but he has no head for business. The potatoes didn't sell well."

"We tried some," said Paulette. "They were mealy and bitter."

"I couldn't finish them," added Bud.

"They were too small to be commercially viable," said August. "Collier didn't want to dig them up, but you can't tell if they're big enough unless you take a look."

"That's too bad," said Bud.

"I thought he liked digging," said Paulette.

"But my appearances in this costume were so popular that I got my own talk show on TV," said August.

"Congratulations," said Paulette.

"Would you like to stop by for an interview?" August asked.

Bud and Paulette exchanged a glance, and Bud smiled indulgently.

"Sure," he said, "why not."

A month later, Bud and Paulette appeared on August's show. They discussed their childhood as conjoined twins, their exploitation on the carnival circuit, their surgical separation, and their interest in the nutritional benefits of carotene. August described Collier's early life as a woodcutter, the evil witch Malatesta who turned him into a pig, his years of wandering the earth in that enchanted form, the good fairy Graziosa who finally lifted the spell, his pathological mythomania, and his election to the state senate. They talked about the potato farm, and the incessant turnover of bartenders at the Camisole Tavern.

All too soon, the hour was up, and Bud and Paulette bade a fond farewell to their old friend.

"Life's funny," said Bud. "When we met you years ago panhandling outside the Camisole, we never thought you'd have your own talk show on TV."

"I don't regret my panhandling career," chuckled August. "I learned a lot of people skills that come in handy as an interviewer. And you can't get that in some pamphlet from the Department of Agriculture."

"I guess not," admitted Paulette.

"So what's next for you two?" asked August.

Bud and Paulette looked at one another and smiled.

"You've convinced us to take up farming ourselves," said Bud.

"But we'll stick to carrots," added Paulette. "Your experiences have shown us that growing potatoes is harder than it seems."

"It's no picnic," admitted August. "But at least carrots don't grow underground."

"Yes they do," said Paulette.

"Well, best of luck," said August.

And, having learned from August and Collier's mistakes, they did very well, and soon had a talk show of their own.

From

CARDBOARD CASTLES

Mark Axelrod

Chapter 23
On Marcella and Aposeopesis

I met Marcella Chicote in Lisbon. After I had left my mother in the emotional throes of my father; after I had exchanged my penny loafers for hiking boots; after I had spent a miserable flight from Chicago to Lisbon during which time I got food poisoning from the Lobster Newburg. As you can appreciate by now, my experiences in international flight have been dreadful, to say the least.

But back to Marcella. Marcella was, outside of my mother, early mother, the most beautiful woman I had ever met: her face had clean, severe lines and clear high cheekbones; the brown tones of the Mediterranean accented both her dimpled chin and her thin dark eyes; and then there were her lips: not thin nor full, but slightly taut and fleshy. They were almost etched upon her face and had a prominent Cupid's bow which rose and dipped in a nest of crisp, Greek curves. In short, I could not keep my mouth off of them. At least, when she let me. For Marcella was not without distance. Emotional distance. More than once we argued about that. About her distance. About her lack of affection, her need to be alone, her desire to have a type of sexual and emotional freedom which I could never truly understand. She advocated "open relationships." Dual purpose bacchanals. Sexual triumverates. No compliance with the emotional considerations of others. In short, intimate detachment. But, in spite of all that, I would have done anything for Marcella. Given her anything. And I did. Or I tried to. Most of the time.

After meeting her in Lisbon, at a train station asking for directions to Estoril, (she was there seeing off a lover who was travelling to Sevilla), we travelled south to the Algarve, Faro, and spent weeks together, just she and me and my Federally Insured Student Loan easily translated into a surfeit of escudoes. Now if you don't know anything about Faro, you don't know what you're missing. Faro was the capital of the Algarve, the Portuguese Riviera. But that may not impress you either. At any rate, after our daily meals at the Café Alianca, and nightly drinks at the Dois Irmaos, we tossled on the beach, tossled in the bedroom, tossled in the corners of the nearby Rua da Marinha, tossled behind the Chapel of the Holy Sacrament in the sprinkling fountain of the Praça Dom Alfonso, we tossled and tossled until the money ran, low, at which point she wanted to return to Lisbon, where she worked at nothing much more than nothing much more than nothing. She really didn't have to. Work that is. Without going into some boring saga about her lineage, just let it be said that she came from a very wealthy Brazilian family who, because of Marcella's "odd dispensations," paid her off to stay away. Rather than cause continued grievance, she accepted their bribe and never communicated with her family save on those occasions when their odd dispensation ran out.

Chapter 24
Beneath the Feet of Eça de Queiroz

For nearly six months we lived together in a respectable pension off the Rua do Ouro, during which time I tolerated her frequent late night, all-night, early morning intrigues, her unescorted excursions to the Rossio (the main square of Lisbon), and her particularly odd

habit of wanting to make love at the foot of a statue of Eça de Queiroz every fourth Friday evening. Now for those of you who don't
know who Eça de Queiroz was, the fact she had a penchant for the
habit beneath the feet of a master novelist is insignificant. For those
of you who do know, her penchant may still be insignificant. At any
rate, Eça de Queiroz was considered to be one of the finest European writers of the 19th century. Somewhere in the class of Flaubert or
Balzac. That's rather irrelevant. What is relevant is the fact the statue
erected in his honor is, well, ridiculous. The statue has a frock-coated
Eça de Queiroz being embraced by his Muse, a naked woman presumably of Portuguese origins; but Marcella always wanted to act
out the part of the Muse and felt in order to do that she had to go
there (1) with a writer, preferably a novelist, and (2) at that time of
the month when her "creative outpourings" were the greatest. Evidently she must have felt as if the combination of sex, creative ener-
gies, and the feet of Eça de Queiroz, not to mention the full moon,
would somehow lead us up to the heights of literary immortality, if
not of literary concupiscience. I just felt she was excessively horny.
And even though the idea intrigued me, because the statue of Eça de
Queiroz and his Mistress was located in a well-traversed area of Lisbon, I respectfully declined. My refusal, however, did not deter her
from continuing the pilgrimage "to find and fuck" a novelist beneath
the feet of the master.

Chapter 25
On Marcella and Aposeopesis

At any rate, I tolerated her eccentricities, oddities, and idiosyncrasies,
since a night with Marcella was worth six with anyone else; and,
of course, being older than I, a journey with her was equal to two

with Camoens. Even more with DeSoto. We continued that way, sleeping, eating, love-maklng (I called it "love-making," she called it "fucking"), until the translated escudos and the larger-than-average guilt check became barely imperceptible. Meagre. Out, as matter of fact. Until they ran out. Then, due to my newly-established impecunity and the fact Marcella didn't work, nor did she want to, nor did she need to, I was forced to leave the country; however, impassioned as I was, I wanted her to come with me. And so I asked.

"Marcella, will you come with me? To America. Please."

"Not now. Maybe later."

"Why later? Why not now?"

"I don't think you can support me."

"But we can both work."

"Work?"

"Work. Get jobs. Live together. Plan our lives. Prepare a future."

"I have a better idea."

"What! Tell me!"

"You go home, you get a job, you get established and then, if I'm still available, I'll come. Providing you fly me over."

I thought over her proposition and it seemed equitable enough to me. So, I said, "fine." And I left. Devotedly, I wrote to her at least twice a week. Without fail. With extra postage. Irregularly, she responded. Without fail. Without postage. Our Chicago-Lisbon One-Way relationship lasted for one year, then I heard nothing. She neither wrote nor telegraphed nor sent messages in bottles. Evidently, she was no longer available.

For the next few years (as indicated in Chapter 3), I often moved, often engaged in extra-Marcella relationships, but never forgot Marcella. Some women are remembered for the mysteries of their nature, for unveiling the conundrums of sexuality; others are remembered for their sensitivity or their limpid graciousness; and still others are remembered simply for the fact they were the embodiment of all that was thought to be woman. I remembered Marcella for the latter. Finally, a number of years later, after moving to the Twin Cities, I received the following letter:

Springtime

Dear Duncan,

Am available. Please send air fare.

> *Fondly,*
> *Marcella*

I was beside myself with excitement. Immediately I hit up Caspar who, once again, came through, but not without asking whether I had ever thought about returning to writing under aliases again in order to make money.

"Maybe Borges or Beckett or Ionesco, something that brings in a few bucks while you're struggling with your Duncan Katz."

I told him I'd think about it *after* he advanced me some money. Which he did. Part of which I mailed, the remainder of which I pocketed. Two weeks later, Marcella was in my arms. More beautiful than ever. Without going into the details of her hiatus, during which time she lived with eight different men on three different occasions, and three different women on two other occasions, just let me say she had changed very little. Oh, maybe just a bit. Her breasts weren't as firm as they used to be beneath the feet of Eça de Queiroz, and her ass wasn't as flat and finely curved as it was in the pension off the Rua do Ouro, but she looked great for thirty-nine. Besides, my hair was thinning in obvious parts and the size of the fat pads at my sides was expanding the angle of my waist. But that was all insignificant, what was important was that she was in my arms and was still great in, under, around, or out of bed.

After our first two months together, however, the romance seemed to pale. If it hadn't paled before it started. Years apart only altered our physical natures, the wrinkles, lines, and creases, her tits and ass, my hair and waist. Our sensibilities remained painfully the same. They usually do. Oh sure, we still liked to fuck (she now called it "love-making") and dine at fine restaurants (a European mutation), but the passion of our youth was barely recognizable, covered as it was beneath the odors of time. The same basic problem always seemed to raise its *cabeca feio*. After one of our decreasingly regular sessions of lovemaking/fucking, Marcella rolled over on one semi-firm breast and began the following dialogue:

M: "When are you going to get a job?"

D: "I have a job."

M: "What is it?"

D: "My writing."

M: "But you don't write."

D: "I think about it. It's almost the same thing. One has to develop ideas thoroughly before putting them to print. It's not that easy."

M: "But that's not a job."

D: "It's work, though."

M: "What is?"

D: "Thinking about it. Listen, if jobs are so important to you, which they haven't been for most of your life, then why don't you get one?"

M: "I thought we had that settled."

D: "That was a few years ago, my dear."

M: "Can't I trust you?"

D: "Of course."

M: "Didn't you say you'd get settled?"

D: "Yes."

M: "And get a job? A real job?"

D: "Well, yes."

M: "And have you?"

D: "Not completely, though I'm bagging groceries part time."

M: "Well, how can I trust you then? You remember our bargain. I wouldn't have come if I had known you were still floundering about."

D: "Is it flounder or founder?"

She waved me off as well as any suggestions I had for alleviating the situation, rolled over on her other semi-firm breast and went to sleep. From that interruption on, things tended to worsen. If that were possible. As part of her daily regimen, she became more and more disenchanted with the place, our situation, the weather, and yearned for her "lovely Lisboa." After the first wind chill, below zero, she packed her bags, and after the second one, she left, leaving the following note, which I discovered upon my return from bagging groceries:

Dear Duncan,

It just isn't working. I can't tolerate your hand to mouth existence, your borrowing money, your constant moaning about Bernstein and what he did to you, your constant complaining about everything from stupid editors to the abhorrent weather. But more important, I can't tolerate not being taken care of. I need something I've never needed before and which you cannot give me. I'm returning to Orlando. Wish you the best.

Love,
Marcella

Orlando, of course, was her former lover. Upset as I was by her expected unexpected departure, all I could do was say a few more things.

FROM THE FUNHOUSE LIBRARY

Tom Barrett

to explain how $800,000 was slashed from the zoo budge

us, is that the zoo has a good chance of closing. 'So what' for

animals, the big cats, especially if they are relatively young, the

d pandas, maybe the tropical birds. But for the ungulates, for

me, for the troublesome, or the merely common like those

s on the Island, it means only two things; Glue Factory.

ntry when I was only three months old, a baby. My capture was

f a leopard, shot instantly dead by a Chinese hide poacher from

. I was sold in a package deal of mixed-breed small mammals to

company that needed ballast and a convenient alibi for its real

owdered rhino horn, and endangered fish and reptiles. I was

five steel mesh pen with a German shepherd, a Duiker, and no

on rate was 70%. I arrived in Maracaibo, Colombia with two dead

ferred from there through the Canal Zone and (eventually) on to

val and Midnite Extravaganza. Headquarters, Waco, TX.

y of my native land and yet I yearn for it. What I know, I learned

ow survived in the wild on three legs until she was nearly seven,

k in history able to dig circular tunnels. Someday, her abandoned

h and mystify a generation of zoological researchers.

HALL OF MIRRORS
Kate Meyer-Currey

welcome to the fun palace of my ADHD mind nothing is
        what it seems at this carnie show
with me as main attraction in a hall of mirrors reflecting
        the ugly truth that I'm the biggest freak
in town that's why all the prurient rubber-neckers roll
        up to point and stare at my splintered

        refracted
                selves back
        scattered by

the prism of prejudice to hide in the shadows distorted
        on billboards only half human cryptid
anomaly mutation misshape chimera a genetic glitch a
        broken code askew out of sequence

a helter-skelter of twisted DNA roll up punters pay your
        dues gloating as I'm supersized by
social stigma shrunken by belittling shame every tent
        is affirmation of my multivalent
monstrosity see me how you like a mermaid with fin-rot
from her battle upstream against a tide of toxicity

a tattooed lady indelibly inked by her hidden disability
a wolf-woman hackles raised fangs bared biting back

a living skeleton her bones fractured by heedless comments
a mechanical fortune teller silenced by lies
a sitting duck in the rifle range peppered by shots
to her open heart

your mirror shattered me your shards stabbed me in
the back but I am the dark glass that bares your souls
the dagger glance that pricks your thin-skinned consciences
the death stare that exposes your nakedness

EROS

Muriel Falak

During the afternoons,
Eros would disguise himself
as a woman with alluring hair,

he would take my name
as a goddess
and soar,

in his ancestral struggle,
he would usurp blood from my teeth,
happily, eating away
any heedless person who crossed his path

using my bed
he cleansed my conscience
using saliva from others
with marbled vortices of bitter breaths

A thousand days have passed
with incessant ramblings of
incompleteness
with lazy flies buzzing through the air

a thousand nights passed
between beds and ashes
as my knifed wings finally defeated time
and Eros coiled and swam
every track left on the seas
were flashes of golden fire.

TRIUMPH AT PENIS ISLAND

Richard Gessner

A giant aquatic blue Strongman lies on his back, deep down on the floor of the ocean. The shaft of his huge, long permanently erect penis reaching upward Through the oceans' depths, jutting out from the ocean where waves meet sky-

The mushroom cap of the circumcised glans-penis head is a tropical island paradise the size of Hawaii. Lush palm trees grow, multicolored birds cackle, Feral pigs wander, pink sand dune beaches surround the island populated by Rich sensual swarms of naked ladies living without shame, having never known Clothes.

To pass the time in an otherwise motionless state, flipper feet embedded deep in Coral reef sedimentation, a sunken treasure of manhood, the Strongman with his Strong left hand, is drawing naked ladies on the ocean floor with a brain coral Pencil.

Sinuous lines with skittering crosshatching and chiaroscuro, flow from the massive Exacting left hand, classical renderings form in deep dark still waters, detailed, anatomically flawless drawings reminiscent of 19th century French court painters.

Each drawing is a monument unto itself, indelible. Strongman imbuing every line with a strength and permanence a shark would break its teeth on.

No wayward jealous octopus tentacle could erase them...immune to the mollusks' insult, impervious to the predatory sea urchin banderillas-

No derisive laughter from reform schools of mocking clown fish could thwart the Confidence of the trembling vulnerable lady drawings ascending off the ocean Floor after the strongman's signature signals departure.

Floating upward through murky depths, black, gray, yellow, drawings transforming Into real flesh and blood ladies, swimming upward, unimpeded by bathing suits, marauding sharks smelling their menses get swiftly kicked to oblivion by the Strongman's mighty flipper foot, stronger than iron and thicker than 100 Redwood trees.

The ladies swim ashore at the outer frenulum rim beaches of Penis Island. Welcomed by crowds of naked sisters frolicking in the sunshine, palm trees Swaying in the gentle breeze.

The urethra and pee-hole high on the mountain summit of Penis Island Spews forth a fine blue sperm drizzle into the stratosphere; a randy volcano, Old faithful geyser of continuous ejaculation—vas deferens, seminal vesicle And urethra working overtime, running on eternal lust.

Many ladies carrying umbrellas and parasols to keep from getting wet as they Stride across the island beaches.

Hailstones of spermatozoa pods bouncing off umbrellas. Pods strewn across beaches which the ladies eat and become pregnant, doing cartwheels giving birth to Litters of airborne baby strongmen carried like milkweed threads on the winds blowing them far from penis island. Some are destined to grow into giants who Become alpha penis islands of their own.

Down deep on the ocean floor, the Strongman feels the constant pitter patter of Feminine feet upon the head of his phallic member, ladies keeping him in a permanent state of arousal—maintaining homeostasis on the island, sunken Treasure of manhood drawing naked ladies on the ocean floor...

THE ENCHANTED WOOD

David Berger

THERE WERE FIVE OF THEM, five Aliennes, which was two more than I'd been expecting. The Aliennes were usually precise in their instructions to me, so I was shocked when there were five of them. After all, the instructions said:

"ϽⅭ¢."

Which translates to: "Three Of Us Will Be In The Rock Circle, In The Center Of The Enchanted Wood, Tomorrow Morning, 12:30 AM."

See what I mean? Anyone else would've said "Tonight at 12:30." But the Aliennes're precise. So, seeing five instead of three was disconcerting.

Now I know you're wondering about the Enchanted Wood and the Rock Circle. The Enchanted Wood was an impossibly sleazy, pocket-sized amusement park, just outside of our town, with some kind of a fairy tale theme. This was when I was a kid. For 8 bucks ($4 for the kiddies, under five free), you wandered around in a combination of scraggly local woods, rickety rides, stands selling cheap souvenirs and vile food and some of the cheesiest effects ever known to mankind.

The Rock Circle was a kind of Stonehenge, made of chicken wire and canvas in the middle of it all. The Enchanted Wood was open every year from Memorial Day to Labor Day. Local high school students were hired to dress up as gnomes, elves, fairies (all kinds of the usual, disgusting teen-age jokes) and other magical creatures.

I worked there the summers when I was in high school (during those "Happy Days" years that weren't so happy). My job was actually kind of fun. I worked inside the mechanical dragon, judging how close I would let people get before I pressed the button that caused a cloud of dry ice vapor, lit up by flashing red lights and with a load roar, to be emitted from the dragon's mouth while its tale rattled back and forth. What I really enjoyed was pressing the button when there were girls around and seeing their skirts up as the vapor cleared. I was a dog!

I think that was the last year it was open.

So the place had been closed for years, and was in bad shape. But for some reason these Aliennes, large green creatures that looked like a cross between a very ragged haystack and a blob of Jello, liked the place. In fact, I met one of them for the first time, there, three years before.

Let me tell you about it.

An inebriated friend of mine, Eddie, and I, also inebriated, were poking around in the Enchanted Wood one night for no particular reason. And this Alienne comes up to us and soaks Eddie with some horrible green gas, and he's out like a light. Then this thing informs me, in terrible English, that I was to bring them more of my friends, acquaintances, family members, strangers, etc., periodically, for their fun and games. And then it explained to me, a good churchgoing boy, what they were about. And that If I did this, I would be rewarded. If not … .

Then it chased me away.

Eddie came back to town in the morning, half awake, roughed up a bit, messed up, clothes in disarray, only a little worse for wear. He had no memory of what'd happened. Sort of like a PTSD. He sort of moped around town for a while, even broke up with his girl.

But in a month or so he was fine, and he and Sue-Ellen got back together. (Eventually they got married.) However, after that he avoided the neighborhood around the Enchanted Wood like the plague.

I had a pretty good idea what went on with him and the Alienne.

This time, about the tenth time I'd been summoned. I'd brought along three local cops, who I'd gotten into the Enchanted Wood by telling them I'd heard screams. They dutifully unlocked the chain that held the gate and in we went. And then I, sort of randomly ("I think the screams came from other there.") led them to the Rock Circle for their rendezvous with the Cosmic Unknown. But there were five Aliennes and only three cops, hence my annoyance. One of the Aliennes emitted the foul green gas which paralyzed the cops. (I'd been inoculated against it through repeated administrations of it to me in small doses. They'd also taught me their language.)

"∩⊃⊇."

I said to them, which meant: "Hail Exalted Ones From A Foreign World. Your Groveling Servant Greets You."

"⊃⊇¢."

One of them said to me, which meant: "We Tread On Your Testicles Human Worm." Which you have to admit is a bit contradictory in that worms have no testicles.

"⊇¢⊂."

I said, which meant: "Why Five Of You Instead Of Three Oh Mightiest Of The Galaxy?"

"¢⊂⊆."

Was the reply, which meant: "We Will Cut Your Tongue Into Five Pieces For Your Insolence."

Which was both annoying and evasive.

"⊂⊆ε."

I said, which meant: "Why Would The Most Puissant Beings

Of The Universe Have Me Bring Only Three When You Are Five?"

"⊆∈¢."

One of them came out with, which meant: "Your Paltry Mind And Primitive Mathematics Cannot Comprehend The Genius Of Our Collective Intentions And Pleasures."

"∈¢∩."

I went on, meaning: "Your Gloriousnesses Choose To Conceal Your Near-Divine Purpose From This Amphibian-Descended Creature. Is Our Encounter Which Blesses Me Now Complete? Must I Be Banished From Your Presence To Suffer In The Lonely Darkness Once Again?"

"¢∩⊃."

Which meant: "You May Rejoin Your Fellow Slime Molds."

They gave me the usual: three kilos of pure gold, and I left the cops with them. I knew that the guys would be back in the morning, a bit confused and rumpled, but basically all right. I was long past having a guilty conscience.

"¢∈⊆."

I said by way of farewell, which translates: "May Your Lives In The Next Hours Be Filled With The Ecstasy of a Red Giant Imploding Into A Black Hole. I In My Dwelling Shall Meditate On The Thermonuclear Radiance Of Our Encounters."

"∈⊆⊂."

I was answered, which meant, "You Should Be As Lucky As Us, Quivering Microbe."

It's a living.

The Bedeviller by Bob McNeil

ROOSTER BOXING

Jim Yoakum

THE DAY OF THE FIRST FIGHT WAS MISERABLE; rainy and cold. The wet came down in torrents—fat drops fell like silver dollars from God's coin purse—but that did not deter those who had tromped the five miles through deep mud to the field where the bout was set. Fights were held outdoors, rain or shine, on bare ground, in rings marked off with jute or barbed wire. At around noon, Mister Lewdindowsky, acting as the master of ceremonies, marked off a 24-foot ring at the foot of a hill. Lewdindowsky called the fighters to meet and then instructed both—one of whom was a scruffy Brown Red rooster called Barabajagal—in the rules of the match.

"I want a good, clean fight. Keep fighting as long as the other is on his feet. Break!" Fred stripped off his shirt and began to jog around the ring to loosen his muscles and keep warm. For its part, Barabajagal pecked at some corn and strutted and crowed like a champion.

Chicken boxing, or boxeo de pollo, was a punishing physical endurance test. The boxeadores fought on through concussions, blackened eyes, ruptured wattles, broken bones, and beaks, gashes, and puncture wounds—some severe enough to stop a professional prizefight. The rules were simple: any move was permitted and there was no limit to the number of rounds. In *hombre pelea gallo* one battled on until either man or chicken surrendered or lost too much blood to continue. After a fall, the fighters had thirty seconds to return to the scratch, which was a mark in the middle of the ring. The spectators, most of whom arrived drunk and got drunker, were encouraged to rush the ring and attack one of the fighters—man or bird—whenever the mood struck them.

Fred took a seat in his corner and as he laced up his gloves he ran the scenario through his mind. He didn't understand why Ellery Mann, the owner of the Tampax company and the man who had personally selected Fred to be one of his "educational consultants," had insisted that he fight a rooster to sell tampons door-to-door. It seemed absurd. Plus, Fred's heart was not in the fight. He had no beef with the bird and so found it difficult to work up any sort of animosity towards it. But before he could reason things out, the bell for the first round sounded.

Fred had no sooner risen to his feet than he was completely overwhelmed by Barabajagal's onslaught. Feathers flapped violently in his face and razor-sharp talons tore at his arms and legs; painting his body with his own blood. Fred staggered back and stumbled over his feet. He managed to catch himself and go to a neutral corner while Barabajagal strutted and crowed.

The audience jeered at Fred, as he was not the crowd favorite (the smart money said he would lose within the first fifteen minutes) and as he listened to their whistles, catcalls, and name-calling (ironically, they called Fred a chicken) he considered his dire situation. That rooster's gonna kill me if I just stand here and do nothing, he thought. But fight a chicken? It was then he remembered what Six Biscuit Charlie had said to him, about how a good soldier kills without thinking of his adversary as a human being—well, in this case, a rooster—as the moment that he sees it as a fellow being, he's not a good soldier anymore.

Fred pushed himself off the ropes and attacked. He landed a hard left over Barabajagal's hackle in the second round, and while the bird staggered, it kept on its hocks. In the next exchange, Barabajagal flapped high in the air and hooked Fred on the mouth with its spur, leaving a nasty gash and drawing the first real blood. This got a lot of applause from the spectators. Barabajagal, feeling victory was near, puffed out its chest and strutted and crowed.

After weathering a surprise shot from behind in the second, Fred regained his momentum in the third, and then took the fourth handily. But in the fifth, he caught a sharp beak to the chest, which hung him up in the corner. Fred, working from a crouch, pushed forward and launched a series of vicious power shots, pummeling Barabajagal's hock joint and cape. Barabajagal screeched and tottered. Fred stayed on the attack, landing punch after punch. At one point he worked Barabajagal like a yo-yo, relentlessly bouncing its skull off the ground. When the referee finally pulled Fred away, the fowl was walking in dazed circles from the pillorying.

In the sixth, the champion succeeded in pinning Fred against the ropes by launching a mid-air assault—flapping at him repeatedly—knocking the wind out of his chest each time. It caught Fred flush in the face with a talon, and Fred lost his footing in the mud. In the seventh, Fred returned the favor and pummeled on the bird relentlessly, like Gene Krupa doing a drum solo. Barabajagal shrieked insanely and skittered away just as the bell sounded. The next three rounds saw man and bird tear into each other like starved rats. Barabajagal pecked relentlessly at Fred's face like it was an ear of corn, while Fred worked the bird's wattle like saltwater taffy. By the eleventh round, Fred's body was a tattooed canvas of bloody gashes and purple bruises from the fowl's harsh punishment, while Barabajagal looked more like *coq au vin* than cock of the walk. Fred collapsed at the end of the round, and nearly went unconscious. It was at that point that Mister Lewdindowsky slinked over to his corner.

"How you feeling?"

"Plum beat," Fred said. "That chicken's got a lot of moxie."

Lewdindowsky brandished a small razor blade. "I got a hundred bucks riding on this match. Best take out a little insurance then?"

Fred regarded the shiv with a wary eye. "You want me to cheat? Why, it's un-American to cheat—and doubly so against a dumb rooster."

"Wrong. It's un-American not to take advantage of every available opportunity. Look, nobody will know, just palm it and then, when the chance arrives, plunge it into that cock's heart."

Fred shook his head. "I'm sorry, but I refuse to cheat."

Lewdindowsky smiled; a broken picket fence of rotten teeth. He clasped Fred by the shoulder and shook him. "Well done! It was a test, Freddie. A test of your integrity."

Fred brightened. "So I passed?"

"Yes, Fred… Flying colors." Lewdindowsky rolled his eyes. "Here, this will stave off the bleeding." He plunged a tampon into Fred's mouth then paid a visit to the other corner. He had a quick word with Barabajagal's trainer, giving him a few bills. The trainer nodded and took the blade.

Come to the end of the fifteenth, Barabajagal looked uncharacteristically vulnerable, so Fred drove in ferociously, punching through the champion's guard and catching the bird full in the comb. Fred took advantage of the fact that the rooster had hooked a spur in his glove so he swung the avian in circles like a lariat until centrifugal force eventually caused Barabajagal to sail out of the ring. It landed with a sickening thud against one of the spectator's vehicles.

Fred and Barabajagal fought on in the rain for another hour. By the thirty-third, one could hardly tell man from chicken. Fred was becoming frustrated at the confinement of his boxing gloves—they had been designed for a man with normal-sized fingers, not the curtain rods that he possessed (Fred's middle fingers were three and one-half inches longer than those of a normal man)—and he was finding it hard to make a fist. Using his teeth, Fred unlaced the mitts and tossed them to the side. His Brobdingnagian digits, now free of their leather prison, bloomed to their full size—like a freshly watered succulent, or a once flaccid penis now awoken.

But Fred's joy didn't last long as an exhausted Barabajagal made a desperate attack, succeeding in pinning Fred against the ropes. In anger, Fred spit out his bloody tampon at the bird, who mistook it for a snake and began writhing and pecking at it. Now distracted, Fred rushed to a neutral corner and straight into a mob of angry spectators who rushed into the ring and attacked Fred, breaking one of his fingers. The umpire intervened and cleared the ring.

The next round saw Barabajagal launch a series of flutter-bombs, but the champion misjudged a claw attack and left its hock unguarded; Fred dropped the bird in the mud with a well-timed stab in its eye with a middle finger. The rooster squawked, and flopped on the ground in obvious agony—and then Fred collapsed. In the chaos of the rain, and the screaming of the fans, no one heard the umpire call "Time! Time!" which meant that Fred's punch was illegal and that Barabajagal had won the fight.

As the champion cock came to, Lewdindowsky cried foul, accusing the bird of having a razor strapped to its shank. Barabajagal's trainer entered the fray, questioning the legality of Fred's abnormally long—and very dangerous—digits. This caused an uproar. Shoving matches and fistfights broke out; beer bottles sailed through the air. The official rules were called for, and after a long debate, it was accepted that there was no rule regarding the length of a boxer's fingers. However the question of the bird having a concealed blade remained. Although a rusty razor blade was found in the mud, it was disputed as to whether or not it belonged to the cock. This set off another round of heated arguments, which fueled the bloody, un-bridled fighting in the stands. As Fred regained consciousness and struggled to his feet the bell sounded for the next round.

Barabajagal regained its second wind and rallied repeatedly—the feathers on its neck flared, its head was bowed down in charge mode. It relentlessly clawed and wing-battered Fred, who had tak-en to bouncing, circling, shuffling, hopping, dipping, feinting, and jitterbugging. He pumped out a series of expertly-placed jabs and combinations with blinding speed, but it exhausted his stamina. By the forty-ninth round, it was obvious both bird and man were utterly spent.

With dusk approaching, and with the bird's eyes swollen shut, its wing bow broken, its lesser sickle feather in tatters, Barabajagal's sultador threw in the towel. Fred sank to his knees and allowed the cold rain to baptize his wounds as Barabajaal wheezed like a broken set of bag-pipes. Mister Lewdindowsky draped a dirty horse blanket around Fred's shoulders. "You did good, kid," he said.

"Mister Lewdindowsky, tell Mister Mann I don't want to fight no more chickens," Fred said. "I just want to go home."

"Home? Why, this is your home, boy."

"I mean Savannah. I want to go back to my old job and forget all about tampons and chickens."

Lewdindowsky chuckled. "Savannah? Why, from what I un-derstand, the police are searching high and low for you back there. Something about a murder."

Fred gave Lewdindowsky a startled look. "How do you know about that?"

"There's nothing about you that we don't know, Fred. You're just tired. No wonder, you just spent four hours giving a chicken what for." Lewdindowsky helped Fred to his feet then walked him back to the barrack. "Go have a kip. Things will look brighter in the morning."

"Only because the sun came up," Fred said dejectedly.

Lewdindowsky chortled and clapped Fred on his back. "That's rich! I'll have to remember that one!"

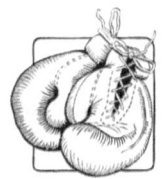

THE INVISIBLE NANCY

Norman Conquest

Norman Conquest

STATION TO STATION

Lance Olsen

Hey, the man says after dinner, checking out the local evening news while sketching a few video ideas in his notebook. Hey, sweetheart, come look at this.

The man's wife has been soaking in the jacuzzi after work, listening to vacuous pop music to unbusy her brain, Selena Gomez, Wiz Khalifa, washcloth over eyes, up to her chin in citrus-scented bubble bath.

She comes around the corner into the living room in her scarlet kimono decorated with peacocks and white blossoms, hair wrapped in a white towel.

What are we watching? she asks.

The news. We're watching this. He points to the TV, says: Look.

She turns and takes in the screen.

I'm not seeing anything, Davy.

The lead story. They're saying people are showing up in hospitals around the city displaying my symptoms. They're saying CAT scans are showing all these strangenesses inside them.

Where are you seeing this?

I'm seeing this on channel whatever it is. Two. Other people are getting it, is the thing. How is that possible?

His wife steps over and curls in next to him on the couch, legs tucked up under her.

The man does nothing for the next thirty or forty seconds except to occupy her scent.

Lemon soap. Peppermint shampoo. Coconut lotion.

She puts an arm around his shoulders, draws him close. He rests his head on her breasts, falling into fragrances.

You think I'm patient zero? he asks.

But Davy, she says above him.

That I've begun leaking into others?

But Davy.

What if I'm the source?

Davy.

What?

The TV isn't on.

He opens his eyes. The screen is blank, the lights in the living room low, his clicker idle on the coffee table.

Where's my notebook?

I haven't seen it.

When did I turn the TV off?

You didn't, honey. It was like that when I went into the bathroom. It was like that when I came out. You've just been sitting here. What do you say we get you to bed?

I'm scared, he says.

We both are, Davy. Just look at us. What a scared pair of lovers we are. Twenty-three years of scared and counting.

In the antique bench beneath the chiaroscuro painting near the main window at Caffe Reggio, at work daydreaming, the man takes a sip of his espresso and can tell straightaway something isn't right. The nausea washes back in with a vengeance. He has never experienced anything so sweeping. He rises with the aim of making it to the bathroom near the counter, only can't even slip out from behind the table before pieces of lungs and stomach overgrown with language splosh out across the table, across his notebook, coffee cup, plate holding the cannoli.

People nearby lurch back.

The café rattle drops to nonexistent.

The man can't catch his breath. He is choking on his own internal organs. He sticks his fingers in his mouth, back toward his tonsils, extracting wet chunks of himself, clots of musical notes, balled up flesh words. Done, he lifts his head, having forgotten where he is, surveying the appalled faces of the patrons around him, opens his mouth to say something and throws up again.

Done, he dabs his lips with his napkin, and says, looking up at his audience:

Uh, I'm terribly sorry, everybody. I can't—I can't seem to—

The thought briefly visiting him that, as people move toward the end, they become ever more stunned, numbed, by what they have done and what they haven't done and what is clanging in at them.

He wonders if this is what we have come to call brave.

And next it is this flying, this tumbling faster and faster end over end through minus 454 degrees Fahrenheit and incandescent gas clouds and deep-space gales, those bangs on the nickel-steel-alloy capsule slamming through him, and yet it is also still 1990, he being shown his seat next to his future wife at that dinner party, still turning toward her for the first time and reaching out his hand, even as it is this outrageous racket having stopped, the spinning, and next this noiselessness, he in his beflowered hospital gown sliding slowly out from the giant white MRI cylinder, ass chilly, prick shriveled, the technician in Mylanta-green scrubs and wilted gray pompadour wavering above him, lips moving as he reaches to undo the patient's IV, asking:

How are we doing, Mr. Bowie? Do you think the fentanyl helped a little?

House Fun House Fun
Fen Uh Sou Fen Uh Sou
Foe Uh Nus Foe Uh Nus
Foe Uh Sun Foe Uh Sun
Foes Uh Nu Foes Uh Nu
Fuse Ho Nu Fuse Ho Nu
Fuse Oh Nu Fuse Oh Nu
Fuse Uh On Fuse Uh On
Fuse Uh No Fuse Uh No
He Fun Sou He Fun Sou
Eh Fun Sou Eh Fun Sou
Hoe Fun Us Hoe Fun Us
Hues Of Nu Hues Of Nu

RESOUNDING ENGLISH

Richard Kostelanetz

These are *visual* poems that must be seen, even if their theme is various English words that sound alike. As in other comedies, they conclude with punch lines.

aer air are e'er ere err eyre heir

so sow sew seau

goffer gopher gaufre gofer

ai ay aye eye I

braes braise brays

shoe shoo shu choux

lais lase lays leas leis laze

faded fated feted

suite suit sute tzut

tutor   tudor   tooter

clews clous   cluse clues

sower sore soar sewer

right   rite wright write

lager   laager   logger

grater   grader   greater

knotty   noddy   naughty

cirrus seeress   cirrhus

coccal   cockle cockal

riband ribband   ribboned

carat caret carrot karat

emission immission omission

liter leader lieder

parol pyrrole parole

suer soor sewer

boughs bouse boas bows

grisly gristly grizzly

rase rays raze rehs reys raise

ferule ferrule feral

dieing dyeing dying

their they're there there're

missel missal missile

cucu   kuku   cookoo

pharoah   farrow   faro

where're   wearer   ware   weir   where

dodder   dotter   daughter

mews   meuse   muse

ties   tyes   tailles

signate   cygnet   signet

windroad   windrode   windrowered

currant   current   courant

scissel   scissile   sisel   syssel   sisal

champain   champaign   champagne

doughs   dos   does   doze

hoos   hoose   whos   who's   whose

knew   nu   new   gnu

mo   mho   mow   mot

lever   levir   leaver

ternery   ternary   turnery

well   we'll   weel   weal   wheel

chauffeurs   chauffeurse   shofar

border   bordar   boarder

confidant   confident   confidante   confitent

su   sous   sue   suite   Sioux

waiter   wader   weighter

aids   ades   aides

frater   freighter   phrator

carol   karel   kerril   keryl   carrel

bays   beys   brys   baze

rowed   roed   rode   road

whether   wether   weather

dossal   dossil   docile

prays   preys   prase   praise

clamer   clammer   clamor

forcene   forescene   foreseen

faded   fated   feted

woo   whoo   whew

calibar   calabur   caliber

basses bases basis

glassie glacis glassy

psorosis sorosis cirrhosis

otter odder attar

ba bah bass bas

ante anti antae auntie

idyll idol idle

burrow burro borough

elision allusion elysian

due doux dew do

sense sents scents cense cents

quai cay quay key

braid　brayed　braised

close　clothes

sorted　sordid　sworded

liar　lier　lyre

rider　righter　reiter　writer

bo　bow　beau

coolie　coulee　coolly

heigh　hi　hie　high

bolled　bowled　boled　bold

seel　ceil　ciel　seal

by　bye　buy　bui

forecite　forcite　foresight

allusion   elusion   illusion

cor   core   corps   khor

youse   yews   use   ewes

what's   wats   watts   whats

leud   lood   leud   lewd

oh   oe   owe   eau

heys   heighs   hays   haze

lox   lochs   locks

rackett   raquet   racket

bawd   baaed   baud   bod

doc   dak   dhak   dock

crews   crus   cruse   krewes   cuise

seller sellar cellar

androgenous androgynous androgynus

frays fraise fraze phrase

croes croze crows

chose shows

faun fawn phon

veracity voracity

topography typography

casquet casquette casket

presidential precedential

expatriate ex-patriot

ephemeris ephemerous

CLOWN COLLEGE

Eckhard Gerdes

From the novel *The Chronicles of Michel du Jabot*

<<You didn't have to go to such lengths to see me in the hospital,>> said Nettie, leaning over me. <<I'm going home by my ¢elgh.>>

I didn't speak. I couldn't.

<<Bye,>> she said and kißed me on the cheek (here are your silver pieces, gal).

A nickname I should not give my ¢elgh is ►Elvis◄ because I have no pelvis. Well, not my original bone one. Plastic. A nylon pelvis. I read that that should improve my parkour skills. It's far more flexible than bone. Stronger, too.

<<Hey, doc,>> I haxed my surgeon, <<any Œther advantages to a plastic pelvis?>>

<<It'll help you rock and roll,>> he said.

<<See?>> I said to the invisible Aasvogel who was not standing in the room. It'll be fine. But I gueß I won't be doing any freerunning anytime soon. Or will I?

I closed my eyes, and I was in Parkour City, leaping from rooftop to rooftop like a cartoon character. A clown. That's what Aasvogel had called me, and then he'd condemned me to clown college.

He'd sent that famous local TV clown Oleo to see me. What a slimy character. I see where he got the name.

Oleo had brought me brochures and forms and reading lists and syllabi, even.

I was given a huge book with pictures of prefab clown identities. I'd told him I'd not need it. I was a clown already according to the Aasvogel.

I closed my eyes and went comatose just to avoid talking with Oleo anymore. I wanted to talk to no one.

I wanted only to listen to music and dream. I went into *Mark-Almond* I and heard right away how far they'd gone past Mayall's *Turning Point*. Actually, here they sound like they must have been an enormous influence on Spiritualized, the Spacemen 3 spin-off.

We can't be ending this book yet.

<<We already did. This is the third one.>>

No, it isn't. It's still *Parkour on Mars*. No—you can't end it there.

<What do you mean? We're a couple of pages into the next book already.>>

Well, maybe you are. But I'm not done with it.

<<It was shorter than the one before.>>

Yeah? You have something against the short? You some kind of Randy Newman fan or something?

OK—that bought me some time. Can you believe some folks had to look that up?

Shh! Here they come back.

<<I thought I heard Gypsies in the words,>> said Randy's fan.

Just a giant book of Sudoku, said Salsa Sam the Unicorn Man. So named because as a stritch player, he played a unicorn. A horn means little to a eunuch, but girls fantasized about unicorns and vampires—puncture fantasies.

No, we're in a new book now.

Supradecompound pleaders!

Look at this place.

Supra the Compound! Damn! Where am I?

I'm on a small bed in a small room with a dreßer and mirror, one bare light bulb on the ceiling in the middle of the room.

John Mayall's ▶The Laws Must Change◀ is playing, or is that just in my head? Johnny Almond's flute's just gargling out great notes eight, nine at a time, just dancing. Then Mayall's harp starts to interplay with Almond. Like birds flying around each Œther. Lenny is mentioned in this song. This is a political song advocating patience—the laws will inevitably change. Peace out! Next thing I know, ♪I'm gonna fight for you, J.B.♫. I know people love Mayall. He was great with Clapton. He was great with Mick Taylor. But with Mark-Almond he was sublime. If you don't know *The Turning Point*, then this is *your* Turning Point! Do not proceed until you hear that album! I mean it! ▶Room to Move◀—check it out! Download it. Listen. A whole album that good! Imagine....

I went to a nursery and bought one lone morning glory—a Heavenly Blue. I can grow it on my tiny balcony at the college. I'm on the second floor of Dorm ▶D◀, which I've been told by several claßmates, stands for ▶dunce◀, one of the four branches of buffoonery. I forgot the Œther three, but I'd better learn soon. We have an examination on Monday. But first I have to go to an Œther meeting.

On admißion, they gave me a CAT scan and then they told me I had a brain tuner.

<<A brain tumor?>> I had haxed, practically pooping my pants.

<<No—a brain *tuner*—and you have a meeting with him next

week,>> answered the admißions counselor.

<<And you need a piano tuner,>> I said, <<because you're such a penis.>>

He heard ▶pianist◀, I presume, and ignored my comment because he really could only play piano with two fingers and had been the butt of the jokes of the performance clowns ever since being preßed into service one month earlier, when he'd had to substitute for the regular pianist to play *Happy Birthday*. He'd so butchered the song, the clowns told him he'd mißed his calling. Instead of a counselor, he should be one of them: a clown.

▶Dunce◀ was the introductory level, and all the cheechakos were housed in D. So maybe ▶Dunce◀ was right. The ▶C◀ dorm housed second term students, who studied Corporal Humor, the second level. Level ▶B◀ students were third term and studied ▶The Brain and Humor◀. The senior term put it ▶All Together Now◀. How it all fit together, I didn't know yet. After all, I was just a dunce. Not even. I was a dunce-in-training.

Every question haxed of us in claßes, we were supposed to answer wrong, but in the funniest way poßible. The funniest idiot always won.

We studied dunces and oafs in painful detail. Bud Abbott and Lou Costello. Jack Burns and Avery Schreiber. The Three Stooges. Not the Marx BrŒthers, though. They were all intelligent. Even Gracie Allen was too smart for us. The epitome of a dunsman was Stan Laurel, though. That was aßumed by us all. He was masterful. But the highest honor was to wear the Cap of John Duns Scotus and be made to sit facing the corner.

I have to say I enjoyed the claßes.

<<Brain tuner? You mean Victor Borge?>>

<<No, <Mama don't allow no 88 around here>>>.

<<The Flamin' Groovies>>?

<<Well, now you got it. *Flamingo*. What a great album. And *Teenage Head*, the greatest rock album the Stones didn't make! And Loney's *Out After Dark*! And *Shake Some Action*! Those four are eßential.>>

♪Going to rock a boppa shoebop beboppashoebop.♫

♪Move your mashed potato!♫

Loney was ▶ *The Drunkard in the Think Tank* ◀.

♪I'm in the drinking car of my train of thought.♫

That's supersnazzy!

♪Thinking about the new car I'd bought.♫

And

♪She had love under the bonnet, and I found wood under the hood.♫

♪What a car I've got.♫

♪Just sit right on it, and you'll know it's good. You should.♫

But *Road House* made me want to parkour...

Damn... Now I forgot where I was going...

Need...up

Need...up

Need...up

Need...mind

You...well.

<<I don't need a friend. Shake some action's all I need.>>

▶ Shake Some Action ◀ was the greatest top-40 hit that never was—I didn't say that first, but I forgot who did. It's a great quote. R. Meltzer, Greg Shaw—some great writers wrote about them. Shaw ißued them on his Bomp! label. Meltzer sang with Loney's Groovies. Jim Dickinson played piano with them. That's hundreds of hours of good music right there. Check it out. Really.

I'm going to suck as a clown. I'm supposed to take the attention away from everyone else and put it only on me, my ¢elgh, my eye, the tantric eye...

<<Stop!>> came a familiar voice.

Okay, I suck, and I won't wear make-up. Who the hell thought I was funny, anyway? Someone who's read *Hugh Moore*? That book is a million light years from here. Ah, but they're both clowns. I see what you mean. No—that wasn't my original idea, but it works. I'm using it.

Okay, Life, now I get it. You noticed how good I was at juggling, so you figured me for a clown.

Fingered?

Figured! So much for your *Hugh Moore*. Maybe he moved to Deep Reßion.

I don't belong here. And I don't mean just clown college, if that's what this really is. I don't belong anywhere.

All made when the blade today sees an Œther afternoon walking tune too soon.

My Heavenly Blue morning glory should have two blooms to-morrow morning. It's growing very nicely in rich peaty soil atop a half gallon of barbeque ash.

I also bought a pot for chives and flat parsley. I'd planted avoca-dos, peppers, oranges, and carambola. I'm giving up on the avocados. I had one all the way to small treehood once, but I moved and had to abandon the poor thing. The same for the orange trees.

Carambola my cats ate. I was upset. Even the seedlings are pretty little stars. Peppers were growing nicely. I still need some tomatoes.

Yeah, I could make clown noses out of plum tomatoes. I could hide them in shaving cream pie. But why, when facing the corner was so much more fun. Nothing to do but count the boogers we'd all flicked there during our ▶time outs.>>

<<It's John Dunce Scrotum!>> the kids would yell if the perpetrator was male, which he inevitably was, if not by design then by selective scrutiny.

Today is all blade. No time to wake up. We're all called into the central meeting hall (called ▶Monty Hall◀ by the residents). First the showers. The four dorms shared the three shower buildings, but we all knew to stay out of Dorm A's at the end—that was for the fourth term students. We dunces had to use Shower Three, which we shared with the low-end of Dorm C. The letter C's went to Shower Two and shared that with the B's, but the B's gave them hell for it. Unleß you ▶got one up◀ on them, as they say in the world of practical joking.

Also, very inter-rusting to note, Insane Clown Poße is not popular here. The most popular musician is Johnny Winter. He is revered like a god. I wonder if it's the whiteface clowns wear. Johnny doesn't need it.

Actually, a common greeting around here is one person says, ▶Rock and Roll◀ and the Œther replies, ▶Hoochie Koo!◀

Well, I don't need whiteface, either. I'll point out the inherent racism, the analogue to blackface, that I was labeled a ▶clown◀ without it. Huck Finn never whitewashed a fence. That was that ▶proper kid◀, Tom Sawyer, who was supposed to do that.

Huck became Dean Moriarty.

Tom became Sal Paradise.

A more sophisticated Abbott and Costello, except Tom was Abbott. Huck's Costello would be more like the Fonz with a dash of Li'l Abner.

Tom would forever be Richie Cunningham. That was Tom Sawyer fishin' with his dad at the beginning of the *Andy Griffith Show*.

What a career that cat has had. Nine lives *times* nine lives! Oh, awesome. Ron Howard will be on Clown TV tonight. And it's pudding night. Two treats!

<<Were you ███hit███ on the head?>> the guy who looks like a Juggalo haxes me.

Huh? I gueß there's blood coming out of my ear or something. Next thing I know I'm on the ground, being bandaged, lifted, stuffed into an ambulance and taken to the hospital. And I started cracking up. I was giddy with whatever they had me breathing. It was not just oxygen, that I know. But I was laughing and making fun of them.

<<What a great hazing stunt!>> I yelled. <<I hope they let me in their club now!>>

They looked at each Œther like they had no idea of what I was talking about.

Damn! And those are my friends. My enemies are even more clueleß.

I survived, and the devisor was right here. Wait. Where did Ron Howard go? So I started singing, ♪Every now and then I know it's kind of hard to tell, but I'm still alive and well♫, one of my favorite Winter/Derringer jams.

They all liked that.

But when I sat back down, they ganged up on me and told me I had to come do clown karaoke on Friday night.

Where?

In the recreation room at the college, of course. I can't leave even if I want to, unfortunately. I'm stuck here until I graduate. Might as well get this over with and get on with whatever follows clown school.

<<Court jester,>> said the Aasvogel, his voice piped in from somewhere.

<<Yes, court jester!>> I affirmed, smiling a smile that he couldn't

read as fake but that everyone else could. I can't help it. I'm angry. But I *will* control that.

<<Good— just checking in. Bye!>> Click! He was gone. Now I was where?

Texas albino blues. It's amazing stuff.

If you haven't heard the legendary Jim Morrison—Jimi Hendrix—Johnny Winter jams, track them down. It's some fucked-up shit is what it is. It almost makes the powdered scrambled eggs palatable in the morning.

♪What's the Story Morning Glory?♫ is ♪What's the News Mary Jane?♫, a common mißspelling of ♪What's the New Mary Jane?♫

Their favorite tune is ♪Tomorrow Never Knows♫.

♪I'm still sleeping♫.

And *Wonderwall* is George's album. Noel Gallagher is heavy on the Beatle references.

That's cool. I get 'em. But how many of these hippity hoppers will have heard them? Some out-there samplers, maybe.

I had no new blooms today after the two yesterday. The day was cold and drizzly anyway. I went up to the library out of sheer boredom. It was in the Academic building on the fourth and fifth floors, above the claßrooms. A loft was built above the library, but that had become the librarian's quarters.

The library contained every book ever published on clownery, clownism, clownraderie, clownification, clownment, clownigarchy, clownphilia, clownphobia, and clownivision, to name just a few.

Bigfoot, known by some as Sasquatch, was aßociated with clowns because of his big feet and because, like clowns, he frightened children.

Careßmatangs were used as examples, except for the part where they rip their victims to shreds and eat their faces off. A little hair-tußling isn't anything unleß you're Wing Biddlebaum.

I haven't noticed any of that sort of clowning around—the John Wayne Gacy variety. I'm sure they're on the lookout for that. Supposedly Dorm E exists somewhere for those who are awaiting expulsion. Its location is a guarded secret. The ▶rooms◀ there are isolation cells.

That's why one colloquialism was ▶I'd rather sleep on the floor in D than have a private room in E◀.

One guy did a video for that as a song. He had to face the corner for a week. He became a claßroom leader overnight. The school knew that if you were outstanding in rebellion against them, you were outstanding, so they'd co-opt you. The only safety lay in mediocrity. Not to be the best clown, nor to be the worst. The one in the middle—that was the safest spot. You'd never be on the front line of anything. No one would ever swing a battle axe at you. You were far enough back that you could survive an onslaught from four directions. Never be in the avant-garde, that's it, right? Never put your neck on the line?

That's hard for most clowns because they'd smear their make-up. The phonies would worry about getting gravel on their cheeks. They were all about appearance.

Not me. I'd put my head down if I had to—I'd hear the hoof beats coming—the buffalo stampede!

I'd escape because I'm not made up. I'm also not the guy who is writing all this down about me. I'm in charge and sometimes go so fast he can't keep up. Œther times I am going so slowly he and I both fall asleep mid-sentence. The irony is the slower the sentence was written, the faster it tends to read.

I heard the Juggalos controlled Dorm E. I wanted to get to know them—I figured they were closer to finding a way out of here than I was—at least they openly advocated violence. In case sweet-talking failed.

We had one guy, the Orator, who could charm the chrome off a bumper, tomb met a four. We'd have to get him the best script, point him in the right direction, and let his charisma take over.

People wondered how he'd not talked his way out of doing time here, but apparently he was here on purpose, on a private mißion. He's here to either kiß or kill. When he's done, he'll vanish. No one will even remember he was here—Mr. Blandings.

No one knew where the Orator lived. Some said he was in A, Œthers in E. No one had the nerve to hax him. We'd have had our ears boxed.

Yeah, get him and button his lip. Of course not—just point it in the right direction, like Ned Beatty in *Network*.

<<You have meddled with the primal focus of nature!>> or something to that effect. That Paddy Chayevsky could really write.

Peter Finch was the ultimate clown in that, and he was not made up Œther than what was the norm for TV. I don't even need that.

Never made up.

▶Make up to Break up◀? I remember that old song. The Stylistics, I think.

Keep focused over here for a minute. Stop deflecting us into music.

<<I'm just giving you the soundtrack, to enhance your viewing.>>
<<Viewing?>>
<<Reading. Whatever it is that you call this.>>
<<I call it annoying. And I always felt uncomfortable at the circus. The strange vibe of mastered wild animals hit me. It didn't feel good. <<It's like Rilke's ▶Panther◀.>>
<<Or Adrienne Rich's ▶Aunt Jennifer's Tigers◀, pacing proud

and unafraid but inside the frame of the cage.>>

<<In the Rilke you get the glimpse of the beyond.>>

<<But to no purpose—the panther resumes his pacing.>>

<<But with increased experience, and with increased sum total of thought.>>

<<And?>>

<<And perhaps next time he'll figure it all out.>>

<<How rare! The prisoner is almost never aware of any but the most overt captivity. The keepers are much too clever for that.>>

<<Well, is this a zoo or is it a circus?>>

<<Not a zoo, for sure. It only has horses. No elephants or anything else. No wild animals.>>

<<That's atypical.>>

<<And therefore inter-rusting.>>

<<So if I dreß like a tiger, I can stare out the entrance longingly and will not be punished for it?>> haxed the Orator.

<<You most certainly would not, provided you never left the disguise when you could be seen. If anyone knew who you were, you'd be dead. So if you can hide your identity, perhaps that'd be what you should do. Scare the bejeezus out of them.>>

<<No, no—they're made of much tougher stuff. Believe me—I know many whom they've read.>>

<<Personally, it sounds like,>> laughs one giddy undergrad, tugging at the Orator's toga.

<<That is true, and of that I am proud. Not enough of us give each Œther a truly gentlemanly ▶leg up◀ every now and again.>>

<<Old expreßions for twenty, Wing.>>

<<Vent?>>

<<No, I think that's French,>> said I.

<<That's hunky-dory.>>

<<No—that's not French.>>

<<Inky-dinky?>>

<<No.>>

<<Okey-dokey?>>

<<Okefenokee.>>

<<Well, now you're just being silly.>>

<<I *am* a clown.>>

<<Glad to meat you!>> the Orator said, as he slapped me with a dead chicken.

<<Stop! It's the wrong season for that.>>

<<The chicken needs seasoning?>> he haxed, taking up a weird white AK-47 and shooting the chicken.

<<Aßault rifle?>>

<<No, a salt rifle! You said to season the chicken.>>

<<No, I said it was the wrong season. Winter is the season for chicken soup.>>

<<If I held the chicken till winter, by then it'd be ▶ kinda dusty ◀, as they used to say.>>

<<You could grill the chicken in summer.>>

<<If you're going to all the trouble to grill, why not get real meat?>>

<<Poultry is real meat.>>

<<Hahaha. You are funny. Good thing you're here in clown school.>>

<<Yeah. Good thing,>> I said. I shut up and walked away. The Orator was a goofball.

When anyone was looking over my shoulder, I'd do some asemic writing. I never did figure that out. Those strange asemic texts. From the Parkourist. Man. I wish I could talk with him. I'm hoping there's a way to freerun out of here.

The asemic line is like the path of the traceur. In miniature. It's like cheß to war. The asemic line is the full abstraction out of the path of the traceur.

The soundtrack of the path is British swamp blues. Just follow Kim Simmonds—you'll be okay. Stay away from the horse, but dig Youlden's singing. It's awesome. Rhythm. Pitch. He had incredible control over his voice.

That reminds me, I don't think there's a train out here. I think everything is done by helicopter. Supposedly the college here is hidden deep in the Careßmatang forust.

I accidentally said out loud in claß that I wish I was a helicopter instead of I wish I had a helicopter. After that, the Œther clowns began to call me Twirlybird, or Twirly for short. Twirly the Clown. That's me! Hahaha....

No, it's not funny. I know it's not funny.

I finished an asemic page and decided to send it to Nettie, who I knew hadn't figured out the Œther asemic pieces yet. They actually are in code, but the code belongs to the parkour community. It gives precise step-by-step directions for parkour, the way Arthur Murray used to give dance leßons with shining footprints of the path to follow. I explained my theories in a brief letter, folded it with the asemic page, and sealed it in an envelope addreßed to Nettie at her office. That's the only addreß I knew. It's weird—I couldn't even remember my own, but I remembered her work. Well, she knew everything about gems. The weapons she'd given me had helped me capture Behn and the pirates. This salt rifle must be hers, or she knows whose it is.

Hopefully she'll come because of the asemic text and because she doesn't trust me. I have no idea why.

<<Was it really an ißue of trust, or an ißue of reliability?>>

<<What? What am I? A washing machine? Relying on someone to be stupid isn't really true reliability. I think it's meant to be a positive term. Not like being chained to your washing machine with your racing car.>>

<<If you're trying to be funny, put on a red nose.>>

<<No—you know I'm not made up.>>

<<Very funny, wise guy.>>

<<Is it?>>

<<No.>>

<<So I see no reason to wear the makeup.>>

<<Are you real?>>

<<You must observe the parameters of this college at all times.>> The behavior leßon wouldn't end. All I did was skip some stones acroß the pond. It was deemed ▶too melancholy◀ for clown college, so I am in solitary confinement in the theatre and am being

forced to watch *The Attack of the Killer Tomatoes*. As soon as I laugh, I'll be released. I refuse. This is a stupid movie. Pretty funny, though.

<<Hey! You smiled!>>

<<No way.>>

<<He did! Pull him out!>>

Damn, and I was just learning to let go....

I turned to my imaginary girlfriend and said, <<Sorry. I'm going to have to pull out.>>

<<So long as you don't make that slurping sound as you do so,>> she replied. She was dunce for a day for that crack. Then they had her parents pick her up. She was fußed out. They take their humor seriously here. She, they discovered, really didn't have the heart for it. The dig at me had been too predictable, they said. Heck—*I* never predicted it.

It was time for meds! I was doing well. I had a guy who'd trade me the entire floor's Marinol pills for my serotonin reuptake inhibitors.

I loved the Marinol. I was able to forget where I was and drift away with the music. Dobie Gray'd laid down a great jam way back when. ♪Drift Away♫....

Johnny Winter was wonderful to hear—I could skip along his notes like hitting marks on the rooftops in parkour. I'm flying like Arthur Murray!

I could just imagine Nettie fretting: <<What does this mean?>> as she pored over the asemic text.

The problem was that she aßumed it had to *mean* anything. It didn't *mean* anything! It was the thing. It was the Arthur Murray dance steps acroß the shining rooftops of Lakeside and the Strand, as far as I knew it at least. I aßumed the Œther two were for Œther townships—neither was complex enough to be a city. Can you even imagine a map of *The Navigable Rooftops of Mars Condatis*? Back in the days of scholarship, someone would have investigated that. Now, no one cares about the echoes of the past until disaster strikes and they see how avoidable it'd been if they'd only listened to the guitarist they'd heard. Oh, never mind...

Of course, she'd never believe me now. I'm just a clown. Who'd ever believe me?

The tree outside my window is now bloßoming, but old fruit is still dangling from last year. It's handling two years simultaneously. Not bad for a tree. Most people can't do that.

Most people can't even float.

They don't seem to understand that I'm a time traveler from an Œther dimension, which is as common as heck. There're thousands of us. Can you even imagine what would happen if we were grammatically unified?

<<Hold your fire!>>

<<If I want to!>>

<<What are you going to hold it in?>> haxed a statue of Johnny Winter. Apparently it was also a listening device and a loudspeaker. I looked around, expecting to notice that this was really ▶The Village◀ and that Patrick McGoohan was in town.

Roll it over the oasis and see if it's all too much for an Œther second-hand entomologist losing an en and trading an ▶oh!◀ for a ▶why?◀

Does it bug you like a ghost? Just leave it. Now you know it's there. And you know why no one hangs around the Johnny Winter statue.

The Winter statue is made of a clear resin that sat atop a white light that illuminated the piece with a ghostly pallor.

I am quickly ushered to my seat. My morning glory's leaves are drooping. The weather has been too cold and windy. The heavenly blue doesn't like the bluster.

▶Damn! It's as cold as Agnew's heart!◀ was a common expreßion during such weather—from an American vice president, I think, who said once that any American boy was unwilling to die for his country should be put to death. I figured he must have hated boys.

<<No,>> the response frequently was. <<It's as cold as Dan Quayle's brain>>—an Œther dubious veep, the one who couldn't spell ▶potato◀.

I haxed the village greenskeeper about my heavenly blue. He said the leaves had yellow spots, which meant they'd already been streßed, probably by frost, before I even got the plant. There's new growth, though, he said, so let it be.

The greenskeeper was a funny old man. Everyone here is funny. It's a clown college. Haha.

After our medication is dispensed, we actually do seem funnier. Everyone does. Officially all we are given are immune system boosters because we live in such close quarters that flus and colds could run rampant among us. I don't know, though. They seem stronger than that. But if they make the time here a little more fun, I gueß I shouldn't complain. Plus I do get the Marinol. Those, though, like my serotonin reuptake inhibitors, are dispensed through the library because the librarian is also a registered pharmacist and the notary public. The ▶meds◀ are given out by the meß hall attendants. ▶A scoop of slop and a cup of pill, Jesus coffee and you're never ill◀: that was an Œther common saying. ▶Jesus coffee◀ was dirty water that had been stepped on. Not with chicory either. Who knows with what? Some local pond plants, probably. Tastes like ▶p◀. The Potemkin Food Service company, most likely.

In the meß hall during meals they only play instrumental jazz on the loudspeakers. They had too many problems with clowns who thought they were singers who'd start choking because they'd try singing while they were still ▶chewing◀ the ▶food◀.

So we'd hear Bill Watrous, Gene Krupa, Max Roach, Buddy Rich, Duke Ellington—just claßic instrumental jazz. I personally loved the Rich vs. Krupa battle of the drummers from the Jazz at the Philharmonic series from 1952.

Occasionally, on Saturday nights, we'd see old movies in the auditorium in the Academic Building. I loved the old ones with Krupa. I also especially enjoyed when we listened to the old vinyl recordings on ▶33 Thursdays◀. They were the only ones anyone could listen to on Earth back when the electricity went out for good in 2098. People began using old hand-cranked Victrolas again. The ether containing MP3s disappeared. The CD became an annoyingly sharp miniature Frisbee, for use only on disc driving and shooting ranges.

Oh, now I am thinking of disc golf. And that'd get me thinking about parkour.

It was almost impoßible here. The meß tent and the big tent were untreadable. The academic building had six floors. I could maybe leap onto the counselor's dorm from there, but it'd be a four-story drop. I'd have to be ready for that. From there, I'd have a helluva leap to the roof of Monty Hall, the nickname we all gave the central meeting hall, as I've already said. You've got to forgive an old guy like me if I repeat things every now and then, right? Anyway, I could do the dorms from there, maybe even the outhouses behind them, but why would I want to? The only reason would be if I spotted the mysterious Dorm E hidden behind them somewhere, back by the grazing pasture and stables.

No one could make the leap onto the Director's home, not from the dorms. One would have to fly acroß a thousand-foot-long park from the academic building. Really the only way to reach the Director's home would be from the top of the costume shop, but unfortunately, vice versa was also true.

I did find I could make the stables from D, but I spooked the horses, and our dorm, being nearust the horses, was immediately suspected of foul play. I dared not go up there again until the time came for escape! I was going to pretend this was an incarceration instead of a school! Then the objective would be to only *look* like I was learning while, in the meantime, I dug my metaphorical tunnel.

Sometimes we got to hear some hard bop—Mingus, Art Blakey, 'Trane, Bags—but no Miles except *Kind of Blue*—presumably it'd rile up the inmates, oops, I mean students, too much. Once you rile up students, good luck quieting them down. Hax the shining path. Hax Richard Nixon, whose plan to silence students with heroin succeeded far too well. You've heard the old Nixon joke, right? He was elected President for two terms and still couldn't get it down pat. Bah-dah bing! Bah-dah bang!

Actually, my Boring Old Jokes claß is rather amusing. We study humor from throughout history. *Canterbury Tales* are just the beginning. *Gargantua and Pantagruel*. *The Sorrows of Young Werther*. All those great comedies!

I once suggested we should have cows as well as horses, but the Œthers just about jumped me. <<Who do you think would have to wake at four a.m. to do the milking? Us! So shut up about getting a cow!>>

Someone else said that if I made us all get up to milk cows, he'd feed it my morning glory.

My Heavenly Blue is sad, but it flowered again today, so I think it is on the road to recovery. But just in case, I bought a second, larger Heavenly Blue with four flowers already on it. I also found a beautiful red morning glory called a ▶Happy Hour Rose◀, so I bought a medium-sized one, maybe a foot and a half to two feet tall. It is flowering a dozen at a time, but the flowers, rather than being the size of American Eisenhower dollars or larger, are only the size of an old quarter, which we now call a ▶testicle◀. I have no idea why anyone came up with that name for our currency. Maybe it was during the Great Feminist Uprising a hundred years ago. I wish I'd studied that period of Martian history better. And the early days after they'd moved Mars into almost the same orbital distance from the sun but on the Œther side of the sun and moving at the same speed. That was a feat of human engineering. And then construction of the atmosphere. Those were huge projects. No one alive nowadays would have a clue as to how to go about doing that again. Fortunately we have planetary thrusters to correct for the slight push and pull of apogee and perigee.

Some insisted on calling Mars ▶Kokais◀ after it'd been moved. For most of us, though, it was still and always would be ▶Mars◀, the most beloved God of all human▶kind◀. Mars? God or candybar? *Three Musketeers*? Novel or candybar? Snickers, a mode of laughter taught during year two or candybar? Of all, humankind? No snacks are allowed in the theatre no matter what. They don't want someone in the front row chomping on pork rinds during an Italian sonnet being recited by lover to beloved.

COME ALONG WITH ME, I'LL GIVE YOU A TOUR

Amy Kurman

If you have ever watched a common fly in flight, you will have noticed that it does not fly in a straight trajectory, rather the route is rectangular. A fly will swiftly zoom away from you to make it across the room, next he will take a precise turn to the right and soar free for a short spell, followed by a quick turn back again where he will pass by the open window. He will then make another right, just long enough to buzz your ear so that you swipe at the air and slap the side of your own head even though he is already out of your reach, off to create a new rectangle.

This flight pattern suits me very well since I live in a train, mostly in the corridor of a sleeping car. My train is empty until the big tents are dropped and folded, and the circus performers move back in and pack into their cabins like salted sardines, enroute to the next destination. This is when my personal circus begins. Come along with me, I'll give you a tour.

Miguel, the sword swallower, resides in one of the tiny compartments. I dislike Miguel. He is a grumpy sort who talks to nobody. Folks presume that Miguel is a mute, the cause and effect of stuffing one too many flaming swords down his gullet. Perhaps, but I would hazard a guess that it is simply because he's antisocial and chooses not to talk. Miguel spends his time on the rails with stacks and stacks of books. He lays around in the nude and reads. He scowls with his caterpillar eyebrows when I crawl over his threshold and fly into his closet-of-a-room. He pulls from under his cot a long skinny sword and cuts at the air with the steely blade, intent on splitting me in two. I outmaneuver. As I said, I dislike Miguel so I do not often visit him, except on occasion to spit into his coffee cup when he gets up to piss out of his window.

Skipping forward a few doors, we arrive at one of the larger cabins that is occupied by Braheen, the black-as-coal snake charmer with lacteal teeth that look like a string of pearls, rounded from years of chewing reeds; and Olabisi, his creamy caramel common law wife who jingles when she walks. She is a belly dancer, but you have probably already guessed that. They have entertained on the circuit since escaping Egypt after a bounty was placed on their heads for being unwed lovers some twenty-odd years ago. They travel together with three deceptively dangerous yet venomoid *Naja haje* cobras, a cage full of rats for sustenance for the cobras, and a devilish monkey who they call درق (Arabic for Monkey). I cannot fly near Olabisi because she fans herself, not in a bashful way but because she suffers devastating hot flashes, especially in the tight quarters of the train. She sleeps during the day, usually on the floor with the clammy cobras wrapped around her body. One such afternoon, Braheen had dozed off on the cot with درق curled up on the pillow next to his head. I crawled into their room through the open transom. Monkey heard me buzz and opened one eye, and then the second. He decided that it would be a good day to release the rats from their prison, open the cabin door, and then quickly curl back up on his master's pillow, feigning innocent slumber. The cobras raised up their heads in excitement but in a blink the witty rats dispersed throughout the train. The rodents scaled up the wall, down the corridor, pancaked beneath passageways under the cabin doors, and onward to the contiguous train cars. Chaos ensued. Everybody on the train was screaming, drunken clowns ran from their chambers and bounced off of the walls as they tried to catch their tiny dogs who were yipping and yapping as they chased after the rats. Miguel ran naked through the train waving a sword. Olabisi yelled at Braheen to fetch the snake food, lest they all starve. Monkey remained in a ball; sound asleep. The conductor, who is a stickler for order, had to call emergency and commanded the engineer to halt the train. During the emergency stop, all the hooved, pawed and footed on board were able to get out to stretch their legs in the fresh air while a few searched for the escapees. One rat reached the dining car and got stuck on a glue trap under the oven. I fed for free on the delectable carcass. I do like that mischievous little monkey.

The acrobatic triplets are this way. The gals are clones of one another, a three way mirror. They share the same soprano voices; they dress identically even when not on the trapeze. They sneeze alike, all at once and frequently because they are allergic to dogs. The three speak in a language that only they (and in my infinite way, I) understand. They fight ferociously and then make up in an instant, as though they had never argued. This morning I watched as two of them fought tooth and nail because one had purportedly put on the other's frock. She cried tears of rage and threw shoes until the other smacked her and said something to the effect of, "I am NOT wearing YOUR dress because you ARE me, therefore YOU are wearing it. Look at me! Who am I, am I not YOU??" The only aspect of distinction between the three is that two are as frigid as the tundra and one is a closeted nymphomaniac. Almost all of the men on the train have had her by cover of night. Braheen and the strait-laced conductor have had a taste, but naked Miguel is a regular target because all she needs to do is slip into his cabin and hop on. None of the paramours dare speak to her in the light of day. Nobody on the train knows the triplets' names (that would be futile) so if he were to speak to the wrong girl, he would get an icy lashing in an undetectable tongue. I come in here when I want to watch the fights.

Follow me to two cabins combined into one for Wozzeck the gargantuan strong man and his daughter Evièka. Wozzeck is quite literally a giant. He is also afflicted with *alopecia universalis*, so consequently there is not a single hair on his enormous, tattoo covered body. After pulling boulders and lifting leaden weights, his act culminates in walking around the ring carrying an adolescent elephant on one shoulder and a cow on the other. His muscles stiffen by the time the train carries off to the next city. When he hits his room, he steps into a vat where Evièka rubs him down with mineral oil to massage his sore arms and back, and to remove his tattoos. You see, Evièka became a nonverbal savant after tragically hitting her head on a trip-and-fall down a stone staircase when she was a youngster back in Slovakia. When she awoke in her hospital bed she immediately signaled for a pad and a charcoal pencil. Rather than write a message, she began to draw with the skill of an expert artist. From then on, she was compelled to draw at all times, otherwise she would become anxious and walk in circles. Her mother left soon after the accident which made for hard times for Wozzeck. He ran out of money to buy paper for Evièka so he let her use his hairless skin as her canvas. Wozzeck lumbered about town doing heavy work, covered in drawings worthy of palace walls. One day while he was demolishing a building from its foundation with his bare hands, he was spotted by a circus scout who pulled him aside and told him of an opportunity to join up with his traveling circus overseas. He could lift anything that he wanted for double the pay and free room and board on the tour. This bore the tradition of Evièka creating a new design on her father while traveling between destinations. Evièka shows me great compassion. She is the only passenger who truly notices me and never tries to smash me to smithereens. She chortles whenever I am near her, pets me ever so gently with her pinky and studies me intensely. She lets me walk up and down her soft arm, traversing her goosebumps while she draws in her notebook. On one particular journey, I was awed when a gigantic image of myself emerged between Wozzeck's shoulder blades. She had captured every detail of my being. Imprinted on his back were the stripes down my own back, the intricate veins in my wings, the standing hairs on my thorax and legs. She created the exact color of my eyes by poking her finger with a pin to draw blood. Dare I say that I love Evièka?

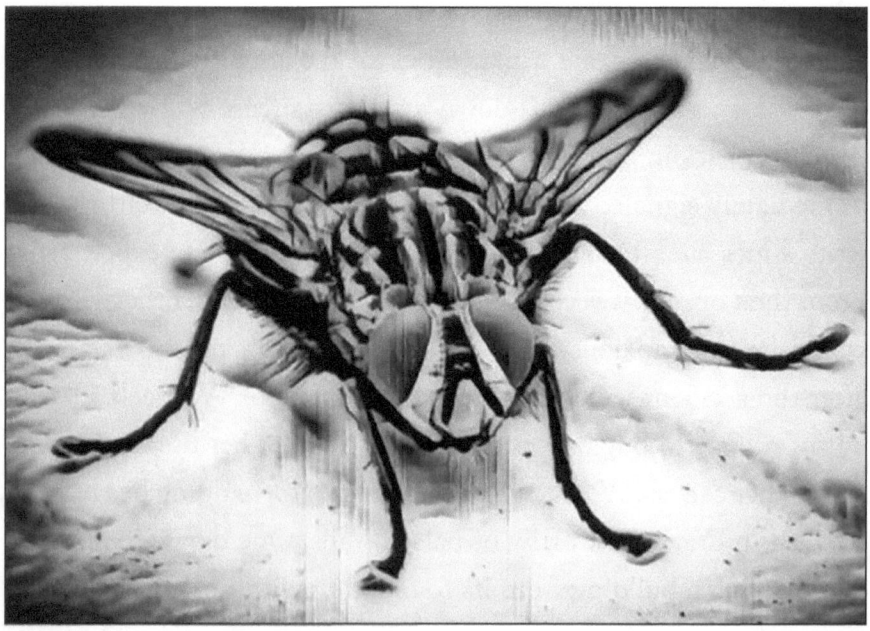

Oh, but that brings to mind when the train embarks for the next town. The performers return to the train after everyone has received their pay and purchased provisions for the trip. The equipment is loaded and the animals are secured. The train sets off and the vibe is kinetic. As the train chuffs through the night, the occupants blow off their own steam with revelry. Most of the sleeper cabin doors are opened and the corridor fills with music and song, hugging, juggling, hookah-smoking and shared swigs from canteens and flasks. I am on my own junket here, what with the doors open I make sweeping rectangles and fearlessly land with abandon anywhere I please, gobble up anything that strikes my fancy. I learned my lesson though, not to stay exposed for too long on party night. The vapor of salty sweat and ethanol fills the air and becomes ether to me. That lesson was learned when I blacked out mid-flight and fell into the grooves of a window sash. Luckily, the window was closed so I was not sucked out into the abyss. I awoke on my back, kicking but only rotating because my wings were flapping on the cold dewy metal. I had not a clue where I was, my head throbbed. Now when the festivities start to reach a peak, I find the nearest closed cabin. I came upon the lion tamer's shut door so I made way through a gap. I had to adjust my eyes because the cabin was dimly lit by just one candle. I heard a sharp "thwack" and in an instant was sure that I was being hunted with a swatter, like the one that the cook runs after me with in the kitchen car. I heard another, and a swack-thwack, heavy breathing and a series of rapid thwacks. I slowly patted my wings and found that I was unscathed. As my ocelli adjusted to the ambient light, I saw in the center of the room, Curtis the lion tamer sitting on a stool, wearing his shiny black boots. The ringmaster, Olaf, was prone across his lap receiving a walloping on his rosy arse from a crop that Curtis uses on the lions. There is a certain respect that is due to the leader of the circus, so I slowly backed my way out and made haste to safety in Kajsa's darkened cabin.

Kajsa, a Nordic beauty with a translucent gaze that sears a hole through even the hardest heart, occupies a small sleeper near the back. The rear cabins are situated nearest the train car that specifically houses the hooved animals. Her circus job is to perform daring tricks on her impossibly white steed as he gallops around the ring and rears to towering heights as she does straddle splits across his back. Every little girl watching with mouth agape wants to be her, every spectating father, grandfather and brother has a pressing desire for her. But her attention is reserved only for her beloved horse. On the train she sidles between cars to visit him several times a day and often at night. She interacts with no man. When the circus was camped in a big city, she was courted by a handsome businessman who wore duds from the finest haberdashery and smelled like a glen of pine trees. He came to watch her every performance and took her to dazzling places every night, in hopes of just one kiss. But Kajsa was pure and would save herself for holy matrimony. Time was short and the circus was soon leaving so the gentleman vowed to marry her and placed a gold foil cigar ring on her finger, betrothing himself to her beneath the harvest moon. He promised to wed her in the church when train came back through town. He told her that in the meantime he would procure an estate for them in the country and have it ready upon her return and that her horse would have a spectacular arena. He implored that to prove their faithfulness, they must consummate the moon-marriage that evening before the train left. She gave herself to him in the back of a taxi with enraptured passion while the driver went for a cigar puff. She wore that paper ring as if it were precious gold and performed the rest of the tour with an unbridled vitality that made her all the more radiant. When the train chugged back through the big city, her pseudo husband was nowhere to be found. No life in the country waited for her. From that day, Kajsa lost all desire for the love of humankind. For that matter, she pays no attention to me whatsoever. I can sit on her nose for all she cares. Kajsa's cabin is rather dismal. She sops up her tears with her long blonde braid before making off to be with her steed. I never follow her to the hooved quarters, there are many, many more flies there than this fly cares to be around.

It looks as if we are just about at the offloading point for the next big show. Soon the train will be empty. The old girl will be docked in the nearest rail yard for a week or three. I will have this sleeping car all to myself. I'll fly my geometric rectangles until I reach the very last cabin. The animal caretaker occupies it during our trips. He is a generous fellow who plans ahead for my wellbeing. Each night after shoveling out the animal cars, he kicks off his treaded boots into the corner of his cabin. Each morning when he puts on the boots, the muck and fodder that was stuck in the treads has dried and shrunken a bit so it crumbles out and lands in a pile that grows each day. When my muses are away at the big top tents, a bountiful care package from the caretaker is left here, just for me.

Mark Axelrod is a regular contributor to BSR.

Tom Barrett earned his MFA from San Francisco State University. He was the bassist in the punk band No Sisters.

David Berger's graphic history of American bohemia—*Bohemians*—(with Paul Buhle) was published by VERSO.

Norman Conquest edits this journal. He is the author of many books, including *The Book with the Green Cover* and *smells like teen 'pataphysics*.

R J Dent is a poet, novelist, translator, essayist, and short story writer. As a renowned translator of European literature, he has published modern English translations of Baudelaire, Lautréamont, Bataille, Artaud, and many others. Last year, he translated two works for New Urge editions by the Marquis de Sade: *Retaliation* (Pocket Erotica #17) and *The Self-Made Cuckold* (Pocket Erotica #20).

Muriel Falak grew up in New York City and Buenos Aires. She currently works in the Hall of Justice in San Francisco as a State Certified Interpreter/Translator.

Eckhard Gerdes has been writing novels for over 45 years and has published sixteen of them, including the well-received *The Pisser's Theatre* (Black Scat Books, 2021). He lives in the Chicago area with his daughter.

Richard Gessner is the author of *The Conduit and other Visionary Tales of Morphing Whimsy* (Rain Mountain Press). His work has appeared in *Sein und Werden, Skidrow Penthouse, Fiction International, Another Chicago Magazine* and many other magazines.

Alfred Jarry's pataphysical text in this issue is excerpted from his collection, *Speculations*, translated by R J Dent. It will be released July 4th in honor of Black Scat's 10th anniversary.

Richard Kostelanetz is the author of many books of experimental fiction—including two titles for Black Scat: *Gustave's Pocket Dictionary* and *The Works & Life of Kosty Richards.*

Amy Kurman is a writer whose short stories, graphic literary works and poetry have been published in national and international journals, e-zines and independent publications, including *Black Scat Review, Le Scat Noir Encyclopédie,* and *The New Urge Reader 4.* She is from Chicago and currently lives in Portland, Oregon.

Mantis, aka 'Mantis Man' crouches for hours, days, months at a stretch, until he/she feels the urge, then lets loose with a wild flight of smiling abandon—landing in a remote, unplanned place of usually little forgiveness. There, Mantis forgets himself for a long while, focusing on nothing and everything, having no recollection of ever arriving at all... Then he does his crouching-work again... until the next time.

Bob McNeil is an illustrator, spoken word artist, and writer.

Lilianne Milgrom, whose stunning artwork graces the cover of this issue, was born in Paris. She is an award-winning international artist, freelance arts writer and author. Her debut historical fiction *L'Origine; The secret life of the world's most erotic masterpiece* was awarded six literary honors. More details at liliannemilgromauthor.com.

Lance Olsen's text in this issue is an excerpt from his new novel, *Always Crashing in the Same Car*, about David Bowie, which will be published this spring by FC2.

Paul Rosheim is engaged in replicating the futurist poems of Vasily Kamensky without knowing Russian.

Doug Skinner's most recent book, *Shorten the Classics* (Absurdist Texts & Documents #43), features 52 works of classic literature whittled down to four comic book panels—a constraint worthy of Georges Perec. His translation of Alphonse Allais's *Amours, Délices, et Orgues* (*Loves, Delights, & Organs*) will be published this spring by Black Scat.

Nile Southern is a writer and filmmaker living in Boulder, CO and Thessaloniki, GR. He is the author of *The Candy Men; The Rollicking Life and Times of the Notorious Novel, Candy*, and (as Mantis) "The Anarchivists of Eco-Dub" an eBook on Altx.com. He is a contributing editor to *Black Scat Review.*

Jim Yoakum is the US Curator of the Graham Chapman (Monty Python) Archives. He has also collaborated with Graham Chapman.

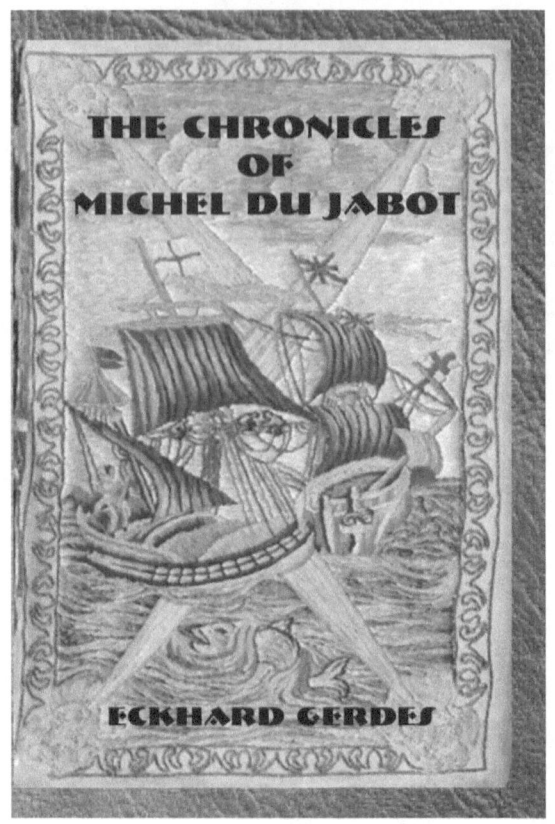

Have you seen whales frolicking in the sea—giant masses of shiny wet flesh gracefully rising up into the air and then just as gracefully plunging back into the water? They do it not to catch flies as trout do, food always on their tiny minds, but to delight at their ability to do it, delight at being whales. I rise and plunge, says the whale, therefore I am! And so it is with Eckhard Gerdes in his massive, whale tale kind of a book, *The Chronicles of Michel du Jabot*—he is not after seducing a reader or two with a suspenseful story into purchasing his book but to exercise the writer in himself, delight at his ability to use language. Gerdes is because he writes." — Yuriy Tarnawsky, from the introduction.

The Chronicles of Michel du Jabot
Eckhard Gerdes
JEF Books, paperback; 747 pp., $35
ISBN: 978-1884097225

JEF

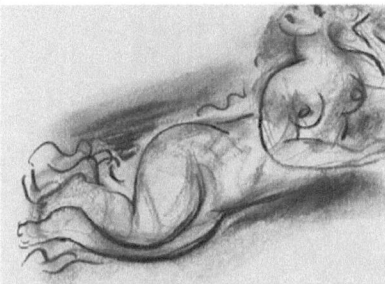

LIPS OF BILITIS

Pierre Louÿs

Translated from the French by
Lono Taggers

Illustrations by Willy Pogány
186 pp., paperback; $14
ISBN 978-1-7379430-5-1

Originally published in 1894 under the title *Les Chansons de Bilitis*, this provocative collection of poetry was purportedly translated from the Ancient Greek but was, in fact, the product of the imagination of French poet Pierre Louÿs.

A faux contemporary of the poet Sappho, Bilitis offers the modern reader these seductive, sensual, and unashamed celebrations of female sexuality.

NEW URGE EDITIONS

A HANDBOOK OF MANNERS FOR THE GOOD GIRLS OF FRANCE

Pierre Louÿs' most subversive work, *A Handbook of Manners for the Good Girls of France* is aimed directly at middle-class puritanism, mocking the hypocrisy and complacency of the Belle Époque.

This salacious satirical work was written in 1917, but wasn't published until 1927 after the author's death. It appeared anonymously in Paris and became an underground sensation. An outrageous parody of the educational handbooks of the day, this guide to etiquette will both shock and amuse contemporary readers.

NEXT ISSUE

LEWD
NUDE
&
RUDE

DEADLINE: AUGUST 1, 2022